Guide to
New Bedford

Guide to New Bedford

Barbara Clayton & Kathleen Whitley

The Globe Pequot Press

Old Chester Rd.
Chester, CT. 06412

Photo Credits:
Authors
City of New Bedford - Office of Historic Preservation
City of New Bedford - Office of Tourism
New Bedford Five Cents Savings Bank (Gray's Watercolors)
New Bedford Preservation Society
Old Dartmouth Historic Society (The Whaling Museum)
St. John the Baptist Church
Severin Haines (Waterfront Historic Area LeaguE)
The Standard-Times

ACKNOWLEDGMENTS

We are very grateful to the People of New Bedford — who take such pride in their city and are delighted to share it.

We wish to express our sincere appreciation to Mayor John A. Markey, pioneering preservationist, who has been the driving force in New Bedford's remarkable resurgence.

Special thanks to the following acknowledged experts who provided invaluable aid in our research and reviewed the completed manuscript: John K. Bullard, Agent for WHALE; Joli Gonsalves, musician, linguist, and tv spokesman for the Cape Verdean community; Richard Kugler, Director of the Whaling Museum; Richard Pline, Community Development Director; Philip F. Purrington, Senior Curator of the Whaling Museum; Antone G. Souza, Jr., Director of the city's Office of Historic Preservation; Cynthia Furlong Reynolds, newspaper feature editor; and Herbert R.Waters, Jr.,Principal of Carney Academy.

We appreciate the research help and support of: George C. Avila, Director of the New Bedford Glass Museum; George Durant, Director of the study group at Fort Taber; the Reverend Manuel P. Ferreira, Church of the Emmaculate Conception; Mrs. H. K. Goddard, Swain School of Design; Elton W. Hall, Associate Curator of the Collection at the Whaling Museum; Ronald Hansen, Director of the Mariners' Home; the Hurricane Barrier crew; Connie and Ron LeBlanc, New Bedford Preservation Society; Francis Liro, Coordinator of the Office of Tourism; Richard McNeil, Executive Director of the New Bedford Industrial Development Commission; New Bedford Free Public Library and staff; Tom Puryear, Southeastern Massachusetts University Art History Professor; Larry Roy, New Bedford Fire Museum; Louis St. Albin, past President of the New Bedford Preservation Society; Paul Saunders, Harbor Development Commission; the Reverend Farley W. Wheelwright, First Unitarian Church; from the city's Office of Historic Preservation: Mary

Ames, Peter Jacobsen, Shelley Wheeler-Carreiro; from the city's Planning Office: Roland Hebert, David Kennedy, Ray Teixera; from the city's Office of Communication and EMS: Jon Foley, Kenneth Sylvia; from the Standard-Times: Maurice Lauzon, Librarian; James M. Ragsdale, Editor; Gerald T. Tache, President and Publisher; from WHALE: Anne Brengle, Mario Souza.

We are deeply indebted to Dorothy F. Miles, author, English Department Chairman, and editor, for her thoughtful review of our manuscript.

And to our husbands, Lee C. Whitley and Raymond A. Clayton, and our families, Mark and Matthew Clayton and Nancy and Scott Whitley, we express our gratitude for their patience, understanding, and support.

TABLE OF CONTENTS

*Starred items throughout refer to points of interest or people about which there is a separate article in the text.
HABS Historic American Buildings Survey
NRHP National Register of Historic Places
NHL National Historic Landmark

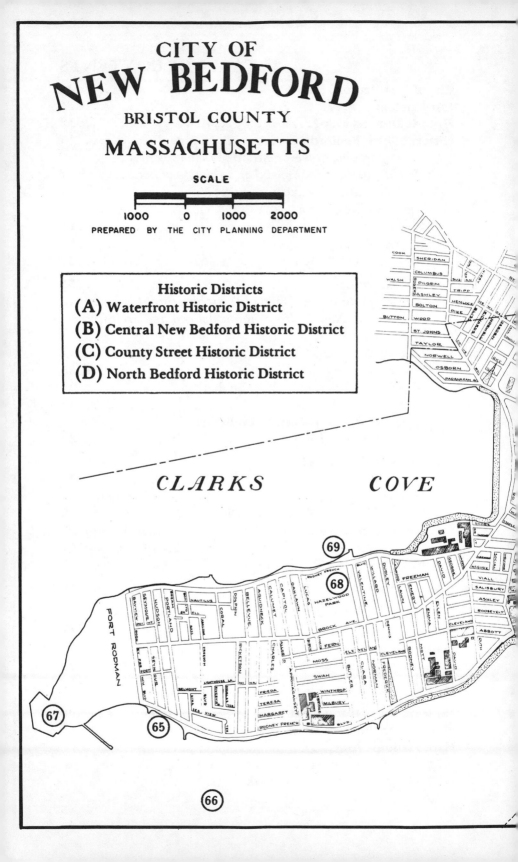

CITY OF
NEW BEDFORD
BRISTOL COUNTY
MASSACHUSETTS

SCALE

1000   0   1000   2000

PREPARED BY THE CITY PLANNING DEPARTMENT

Historic Districts
(A) Waterfront Historic District
(B) Central New Bedford Historic District
(C) County Street Historic District
(D) North Bedford Historic District

CLARKS   *COVE*

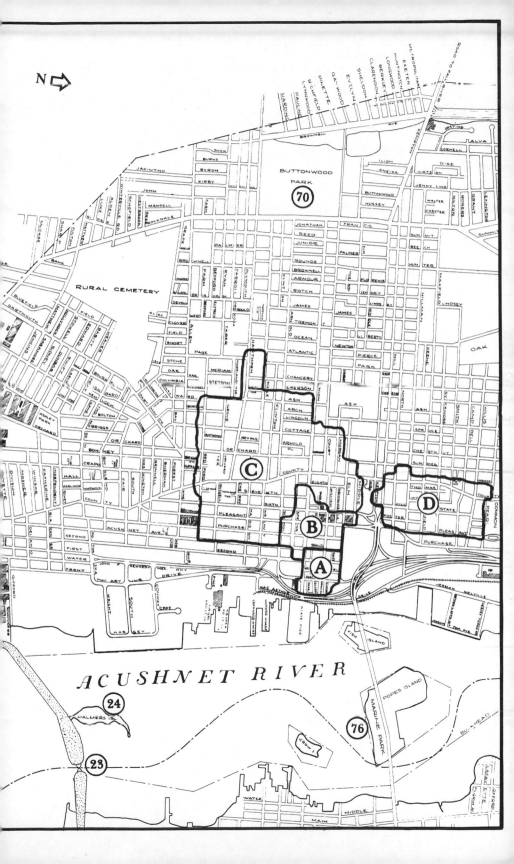

INTRODUCTION

We invite you to explore New Bedford and share our enthusiasm for this exciting, reawakening city.

The focus of the book is the guided tour which leads interested tourists and residents through points of historical, architectural, and scenic interest. In addition, New Bedford's history is traced briefly, yet with depth and insight, to provide a valuable background. This awareness of her past gives the necessary perspective so that her present and future can be fully appreciated. Also, a nodding acquaintance with architecture is included to broaden your understanding and appreciation of the wealth and variety of New Bedford's architecture. It acts as a guide similar to a bird watcher's — to enable you to recognize architectural styles and comprehend their evolution.

Every point of interest has been carefully researched and visited. In the heading of each is found: name, address, directions, date, whether open or private, fee charged or not, facilities available. The text of each includes a description plus the background, history, and architecture of the point of interest as well as the people whose lives have touched it. Scenic and recreational interests focus more on facilities, use, and appreciation.

We hope you have in this book all the tools necessary for your rewarding and exciting adventure in the discovery of New Bedford, whether you travel by car, on foot, by bike, or in the comfort of your armchair.

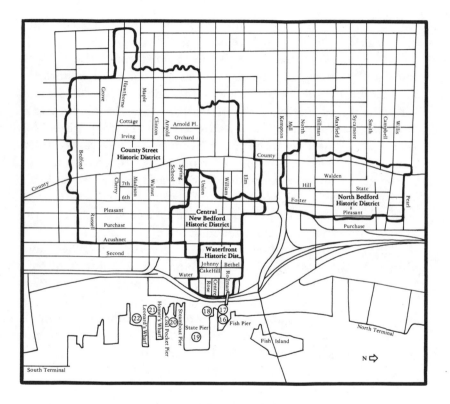

County Street Historic District

Central New Bedford Historic District

Waterfront Historic Dist.

North Bedford Historic District

Grove
Hawthorne
Maple
Cottage
Clinton
Arnold
Arnold Pl.
Irving
Orchard
Bedford
Cherry
7th
Madison
Spring
School
Walnut
6th
Union
William
Elm
County
Kempton
Mill
North
Hillman
Maxfield
Sycamore
Smith
Campbell
Willis
Walden
Hill
State
Foster
Pleasant
Pearl
Russell
Pleasant
Purchase
Purchase
Acushnet
Second
Water
Johnny CakeHill
Bethel
Rodman
Centre
Rose
Leonard's Wharf
Homer's Wharf
Coal Pocket Pier
Steamboat Pier
State Pier
Fish Pier
Fish Island
North Terminal
South Terminal

22 21 20 18 17 16 19

N ⟹

NEW BEDFORD HISTORY

What makes New Bedford ring true is its authenticity. This is not a reconstructed town built with outside money to recreate the past. Rather it is the past, intermingled with the present, still living, still active, and still working. Where you walk today others have walked for hundreds of years. When you enter a ship's chandlery you know that ships' captains and seamen have entered these same doors, buying their same goods for as long as anyone can remember. This is how it has been and will continue to be here in New Bedford, for this is the normal everyday life of this real, working, active, throbbing New England seaport.

New Bedford is a city that takes pride in her past, her present, and her future. She evolved from a quiet pastoral and fishing community to the competition and excitement of the whaling center of the world, then to a leading cotton manufacturing center, and finally to today's historically revitalized community, which benefits visitors as well as local inhabitants.

During the golden era of whaling, prosperous sea captains and merchants lived on County Street overlooking the busy harbor, where docks were lined with whalers and piled high with barrels of whale oil. Then as whaling declined in the last half of the 1800s, the textile industry came into its own. New Bedford moved forward economically to become a famed textile center, her large brick mills humming with the economic heartbeat of the city. Today the textile industry remains an important part of the economy, though the emphasis has changed from making fabrics to making finished garments ready for sale in stores all over the country. Fishing continues to be the backbone of New Bedford's life as the largest seaport on the east coast in terms of catch landed and the leading port in scalloping. The city has maintained and is restoring the waterfront area, which has been in continuous use since 1755. It has also preserved and is restoring many of the historic homes of whaling and textile kings. Few cities have progressed as gracefully or with as much foresight as has New Bedford, which continuously sought new avenues of economic prosperity before a present one was exhausted.

To go back to New Bedford's beginning, in 1602 the ship *Concord* sailed from Falmouth, England, captained by adventurer and explorer Bartholomew Gosnold, who was looking for a better route to America and hoping to establish a plantation in the New World. He entered what would become New England, passing along the sandy shores of Cape Cod, which he named for the ever present codfish. The ocean-weary crew landed on what is now Cuttyhunk Island, at which time Gosnold named all the islands for his sovereign, Elizabeth. From this base he explored the mainland, landing near the mouth of the Acushnet River where he was much taken by the rich, beautiful, and inviting countryside. Though the intended settlement was never completed, he returned to England with tales of fertile land, navigable rivers, verdant fields, and friendly Indians as well as furs and sassafras roots — all of which added fuel to the fire of those interested in trading with and settling in this New World. A wilderness had been touched, and slowly settlers would seek out this land that so appealed to Bartholomew Gosnold.

Yet it would be fifty years before a portion of the land would be purchased by white men. Many of the early settlers who came to the New Bedford/Dartmouth area were Quakers, Baptists, or others from the Plymouth Colony who wished to live independent of Puritan pressures. At this time there was strong persecution of all people, especially Quakers and Baptists, who did not follow the strict rules laid down by Puritans. In 1652 thirty-six settlers, among them such familiar names as Captain Miles Standish, William Bradford, John Alden, Manasseh Kempton, John Cooke, and John Howland, joined together and bought from Indian Chief Massasoit and his son Wamsutta a parcel of land which would ultimately include New Bedford, Acushnet, Fairhaven, Dartmouth, and Westport. The entire area was named Dartmouth and incorporated in 1664.

The early colonists in this area did not settle as a close-knit group around a central meetinghouse as was common among Puritan settlers, but rather set up homesteads independent of each other. There were two reasons for this. One was the many rivers in the area which automatically divided the land and separated homesteads. The other was a strong desire on the part of the Quakers and Baptists especially to avoid a community center where the Plymouth General Court would insist on sending a minister to enforce and encourage the Puritan way of life on all settlers regardless of their personal beliefs. The seeds of New Bedford's greatness were sown by these early independent settlers seeking greater freedom of thought and action. Their descendants, remembering these early persecutions, would in later years offer these same sacred freedoms to other ethnic groups. This determination to live independently and be controlled only by their own conscience and beliefs would ultimately take them from the depths of despair during Indian massacres to the heights of economic success during New Bedford's golden age of whaling.

While Massasoit, Sachem of the Wampanoag Indians, lived there were friendly relations between white men and red men. Yet under the surface hostilities were developing. Unethical white men took advantage of the natives; Indians began to see their land slowly taken from them; and misunderstandings and injustices developed. All combined to slowly encourage separation and mistrust. After Massasoit's death, his younger son, Pometacom, known as King Philip by the white men, soon became the leading Sachem of the Wampanoags.

This loosely-knit wilderness settlement had barely begun to grow when, within ten years, Massasoit's friendly overtones were replaced by his son King Philip's passionate desire to drive the white men from the Indian's hunting grounds. A well-meant incident triggered the final confrontation. An Indian, John Sassamon, one of King Philip's chief advisors, had been strongly affected by the teachings of missionary John Eliot. Learning of Philip's determination to attack the white men, he went to Plymouth to warn them. When Philip discovered this he became furious and had his once trusted friend murdered. The General Court retaliated by capturing, trying, convicting, and hanging the three Indians who had committed the murder. This resulted in open war.

The independent colonists, who had settled on large tracts of land some distance from each other, were at the mercy of the Indians who attacked in 1675. Today one cannot imagine the horror that was felt in the hearts of those isolated settlers as Indians came, brutally killing and mutilating loved ones, burning homes and fields, destroying livestock, and spreading fear and devastation. Those who could fled for protection to three local garrisons: Russell's garrison on the north shore of the Apponagansett River, Cooke's garrison in Oxford Village, Fairhaven, and the garrison on Palmer Island.

As in all wars there were some on both sides who cared about humane, fair treatment of human beings whether adversaries or not, and there were those who cared only for expediency with no thought of honor. Indian fighter Captain Benjamin Church was caught in this age old conflict. He was indebted to several local Indian groups. Little Eyes of the Sagonite tribe had befriended him and in return Church gave the Indians safe conduct to Palmer Island where they were protected. Sachem Awashonks of the Sakonnet tribe supported Church and helped to bring about the final victory over Philip. Then to Captain Church's ultimate regret an incident occured which forced him to go against his personal feelings of loyalty and honor. A group of Indians were encouraged to surrender to the Russell garrison with promises of fair treatment. Instead Plymouth soldiers arrived with orders higher than those of Church's, and he was forced to take the Indians as prisoners to Plymouth. Here, along with others, totaling 178, they were sold into slavery in the West Indies. Among them were the wife and son of King Philip. This enslavement makes you wonder what had happened to our early colonists' desires for freedom for all. Possibly fair treatment then might have prevented further Indian massacres in the area.

Nearly every white settler's home was destroyed, settlers were tortured, lives lost, and lands ravaged before King Philip was killed and the remaining white men were able to regroup, take up ax and plow, and rebuild their wilderness homes. The Plymouth General Court passed a ruling that all homes in the future must be built near each other for mutual protection.

BEDFORD VILLAGE AWAKENS

Manasseh Kempton, one of the original Dartmouth purchasers, owned land along the western shore of the Acushnet River. Prior to 1711 Joseph Russell bought a parcel of this land and with his son established a farming homestead in the area that is now roughly bounded by County, Spring, and Elm Streets and the Acushnet River. Here was born Joseph Russell III, who would be known as the founder of New Bedford. He later built his house on County Street, from which he could overlook the harbor. By the 1750s Joseph III, an industrious, inventive, and enterprising young man, had laid out village streets and house lots and introduced whaling to the already established agricultural economy, thus launching the town on what would be its greatest era. He also set up the first whale oil factory and established a limited foreign trade. A village was coming alive.

To this developing community came caulker John Loudon,

South Sea Whale Fishing

who bought the first lot of land from the Russell homestead and started a shipbuilding industry in 1760. Soon after him came Benjamin Taber, boat builder and block maker; John Allen, house carpenter; Gideon Mosher, mechanic; Barzillai Myrick, ship carpenter; and Elnathan Sampson, blacksmith. The economy was shifting from land-related to sea-related industries. These craftsmen launched the vital industries which would support and work in partnership with the developing whaling and fishing industries. Sister industries such as ships carpentry, rope making, rigging, caulking, painting, blacksmithing, coopering, and sailmaking set the foundation and standards of superior craftsmen who would take pride in their work from early shipbuilding up through the cotton and tool manufacturing of the late 1800s and early 1900s.

By 1765 the foundation was well laid for the arrival of Joseph Rotch from Nantucket, who brought with him an outstanding knowledge of the whaling industry, strong financial backing, and an enthusiasm which gave whaling the impetus it needed. Until this time small ships of forty to sixty tons made six-week to two-month voyages, taking mainly right whales, which were closer to home but did not give as fine an oil as did the harder-to-find sperm whale. The ships had to bring the whale blubber back to port, before it spoiled, to be rendered in trypots set up along the river bank. Here the blubber was cooked over a small fire to ob-

William Wall's **Old Four Corners** *— Union Street looking west from Water Street in 1807 — William Rotch, Sr. house behind poplars — Rotch in chaise, Abraham Russell with cane and William Rotch, Jr.*

tain the sought after whale oil. After the arrival of Joseph Rotch two important changes took place. First, larger ships such as the *Dartmouth,* built by Rotch in 1767, made it possible to make longer voyages, carry more oil, and venture farther in search of the more profitable sperm whale. Secondly, they developed a method of rendering the oil aboard ship, allowing them to bring back only the profitable whale oil and bone. On-board trypots made these longer voyages possible because of reduced spoilage.

Having left his son William to run their successful whaling business on Nantucket, Rotch and his two younger sons, Joseph, Jr. and Francis, came to the mainland looking for even brighter horizons where they could establish a more encompassing whaling business. The Acushnet River provided the excellent harbor they needed as well as an easy avenue for trade with Boston and Newport. Here on the western shore they bought ten acres of land from Joseph Russell III. Today these well known "ten acres" lie roughly east of Pleasant Street, down both sides of William Street (named for William Rotch) to the water, and include a good part of today's Waterfront Historic District. Joseph Rotch built his house near the corner of William and Water Streets, which at that time was known as Rotch's Hill. From here he could look out over the harbor and wharves where his ships lay at anchor.

Where a hundred years earlier forests had met the river's edge, broken here and there by fields of Indian corn and peaceful Indian wigwams, now developed this infant village. Two Josephs, Russell and Rotch, would lead this village from infancy through adolescence. Appropriately Joseph Rotch named the village Bedford after the Duke of Bedford in England whose family name was Russell. Henceforth Joseph Russell III was affectionately called the "Duke".

By 1771 the Acushnet River was busy with whaling ships supporting bustling communities on both sides of the river totaling 321 dwellings, 119 shops and warehouses, anchoring 3059 tonnage of vessels along 30,684 feet of wharves.[1] On the Bedford side homesteads were owned from Clark's Point to the head of the river, but the main village was bounded roughly by what is now Walnut, County, Elm, and Kempton Streets. The Russell and Kempton families lived on County Street, where they combined farming with their seafaring ventures. Joseph Rotch and others connected with whaling and shipbuilding lived nearer the river along Water Street.

At first Joseph Rotch, along with other whale ship owners, sent oil to Boston to be shipped to England or to Newport to be made into candles. But Rotch soon realized that he would see more of a profit if he expanded his business to include these money making functions. He began shipping his own oil directly to England and hired candle makers from Newport, opening his own candle works in New Bedford. He also carefully controlled the amount of oil sent either to Boston or Newport, thus giving him a very prosperous controlling hand in the whale oil business. This greatly annoyed John Hancock in Boston, who had been maneuvering to control the whaling economy himself. Until the American Revolution, thanks to Joseph Rotch's powerful influence and business acuity, the town prospered; homes, highways, candle works, and wharves were built, and whaling and merchant fleets launched.

AMERICAN REVOLUTION

The American Revolution brought economic depression and great loss of property as well as heartbreak and conflict of conscience. Whaling and foreign trade were brought to a standstill as British ports were closed to Colonial trade, and British men-of-war harassed and captured Colonial ships. Here on the Acushnet River two communities, one on the Fairhaven side and one on the

Bedford side, shared the same harbor and the same deep feeling of loyalty to their country's desire for freedom, but they were sharply divided in their reactions. On the Fairhaven side zealot patriots and active privateersmen preyed successfully on British ships, causing great loss to their shipping and angering the British. They willingly took part in all out war. On the Bedford side many of the citizens were Quakers, whose faith kept them from partaking in aggressive actions, even though they lost heavily economically. These were the descendants of those earlier independent Quakers who insisted on living free and independent of Puritan rule. They well understood the importance of sacrificing to obtain freedom. They too did their part through economic and financial support, for the harbor served as a supply center and haven for privateersmen from all over New England. The famous John Paul Jones was an occasional visitor.

On September 5, 1778, the British, not knowing or caring about the individual consciences of the two harbor communities, landed at Clark's Cove seeking retaliation for their many losses at sea. Unfortunately Bedford's artillery company was occupied elsewhere, leaving an unprotected town except for the Quakers who, out of belief, would not take up arms. The British, unimpeded, marched up County Street to the village where they set fire to ships, wharves, and buildings, including the original homes of Joseph Rotch and John Loudon. That moonlit night witnessed the awesome destruction of the business section of Bedford Village. Not a whaling vessel would sail again from the village until 1785.

Though her economy and spirits were at a low ebb, undaunted Bedford Village arose from her ashes and rebuilt. Peace, temporary prosperity, and growth followed the close of the war, and by 1787 the village of Bedford became the independent town of New Bedford. The "New" was added to distinguish it from the already incorporated town of Bedford, near Boston. Whaling and merchant ships sailed in and out of her protected harbor; barrels of oil were piled high on her wharves; the sound of axes and hammers could be heard in the shipyards; and the rumble of wagon wheels vibrated on the dirt roads, bringing lumber for new homes, wharves, and ships. In the Midas world of whaling she was second only to Nantucket.

New Bedford's star was rising on the horizon, but world events were happening that would cause it to dip sharply before reaching its apex in the golden era of whaling. The Napoleonic Wars, restrictions on American ships in British and French ports,

Early dock scene

seizure on the high seas of American ships, and the impressment of American sailors brought on Jefferson's Embargoes in 1807, which all but closed New England seaports. Maritime economy remained at a practical standstill until after the War of 1812.

GOLDEN AGE

By 1818 the conflict was over. Whaling entered its golden age, and New Bedford's growth and prosperity seemingly knew no limits. By 1830 she had surpassed Nantucket as the leading whaling port. She reached her zenith in 1857 with a fleet of 329 ships, over 10,000 men employed, and the industry valued at nearly twelve million dollars. New Bedford owed money to no one nor was she in anyone's debt, for her own people had made her what she was. Her prosperity came from the sea by way of the mighty whale. This powerful industry brought in great wealth on its own as well as supporting a wide variety of businesses needed in its successful pursuit. The source of almost every dollar in New

21

Quaker gentleman

Bedford could be traced back to the sea, whether it was in building a ship captain's mansion, supplying food for the town, or setting up a rope-walk or candle works. Whaling prospered, and the world knew of New Bedford. Her ships could be found on every ocean and her sailors at home in every port.

    This growth and prosperity was due in great part to the indomitable character and devotion of the Quakers. As the leading shipowners and merchants of the late 1700s and early 1800s, they were the guiding influence in New Bedford. Their names could be found on the board of directors or among the officers of almost every commercial company, bank, or philanthropic organization in the town. As a group they believed in harmonious family living, hard work, strict self-discipline, trying to live exemplary lives as directed by the Holy Spirit, complete honesty, simple unpretentious living, and equality and freedom of thought for all. For most towns the three "R's" stand for the rudiments of education, but to New Bedford they represented three Quaker families: Russells, Rotches, and Rodmans, who had a continuously positive influence on the town since its beginning. Along with the three "R's" stood other families — equally important pillars of New Bedford — such as Hathaways, Howlands, Tabers, Grinnells, Morgans, and Crapos. These were the personalities that launched and guided the town through the exciting days of whaling and into the economic boom of the textile industry.

While whaling continued successfully into the 1880s, events began to take place in the mid 1800s that would eventually end this proud industry. As whales became scarcer it was necessary to make longer and more difficult voyages. Where once the huge mammals had been plentiful in the Atlantic Ocean, it became necessary to venture to the Indian Ocean, the Pacific Ocean, the Sea of Japan, and finally through the treacherous Bering Strait up into the very Arctic itself. Here wooden ships propelled only by sail, ever dependent on the constantly changing and unpredictable wind, would brave their way in June. If luck were with them, the crew would take the desired number of whales, render the oil, and, breaking through the early ice of September, sail back through the Strait before the permanent winter ice closed in. If not, then faithful ships had to be abandoned, and as many lives saved as possible.

The first Arctic crisis came in the fateful year of 1871, when over 1200 men and a few women were forced to leave the security and warmth of thirty-three ships (twenty-two from New Bedford), which had become locked in the Arctic ice. In small whaling boats they turned their backs on these once proud ships, now left standing like deserted skeletons in an exposed icy grave. They rowed for several days through shallow, open, icy waters hoping against great odds to catch other whaling ships that were still in open water and had not yet started south. Here is a true picture of bravery, endurance, resourcefulness, and determination, for in spite of high seas, gale winds, extreme cold, and crowded,

MONTICELLO   KOHOLA   EUGENIA WAINRIGHT INLET AWASHONKS   THOS DICKASON   MINERVA   WM ROTCH   VICTORIA   MARY
                                JULIAN

ABANDONMENT OF THE WHALERS IN THE ARCTIC OCEAN SEPT 1871.

Abandonment of the whalers in the Arctic Ocean, 1871

small boats the torturous trip was made without a single loss of
life. However, the financial loss was enormous. The entire
season's catch was lost as were all the whaling ships, most of
which were not insured in any way. In 1876, 1888, and 1897
there were similar losses including ships as well as lives. The profits could be great, but so could the risks and the losses[2].

Along with these natural events came other factors effecting
the once lucrative whaling business. No more fortunes were made
from whaling after 1850. Gold was discovered in California in
1849, causing many seamen to desert their ships in search of the
ever inviting get-rich-quick fever. Whaling was so successful in
the peak year of 1857 that a year later, as bountiful catches continued, the market became flooded, and prices dropped
dramatically. From then on the price trend of whale oil, though
fluctuating, went progressively down due to overstocked markets
and the discovery of petroleum in Pennsylvania in 1859. At the
same time a continual rise in the price of whalebone helped tem-
porarily to offset the declining whaling economy. The Civil War
also took its toll on the whaling industry. Many ships were captured or sunk during the war. Others were used as part of the
famous "Stone Fleet", sunk to blockade the harbors of Charleston
and Savannah. Then last but far from least were the natural
elements that took their own toll, such as hurricanes, coral reefs,
and even the cornered whale itself, who could turn sturdy ships

into kindling wood with one mighty blow. Seeing the writing on the wall, the foresighted New Bedfordites wisely began to shift the emphasis of their economy from whaling to new industries.

The mid-1800s saw the economic emphasis gradually swing back from sea-related to land-related industries. Along with her economic changes and growth she also reached political maturity on March 18, 1847, with the signing of a city charter and the election of her first mayor, the Honorable Abraham H. Howland. The new government was supported by six aldermen and twenty-four city councilmen, led by James B. Congdon as first city council president. With wisdom, compassion, and outstanding business sense, Mayor Howland successfully led his compatriots from the golden age of whaling into the early era of what would prove to be the even more prosperous industrial age.

NEW BEDFORD'S INDUSTRIAL AGE

Mills and factories soon became a new way of life, which allowed the economic lifeblood of New Bedford to flow unimpeded. Even as whaling was still flourishing, foresighted businessmen saw the value of additional industries for the city. Fabrics were doing well in other parts of New England, why not in New Bedford where the damp ocean climate was ideal for making cotton fabrics; where there was a ready made port for shipping; and there was sufficient manpower to train and capital to invest? Though the immediate returns would not be as great as in whaling, the risks were less, the life expectancy greater, and the overall economic view encouraging for long term capital gain.

The stage was set: two descendants of the well-known Howland family, Thomas Bennett, Jr. and the Honorable Joseph Grinnell, joined forces to play the leading roles in setting up Wamsutta Mills, the first successful textile mill. In the 1840s mechanically talented Thomas Bennett, Jr., realizing the economic possibilities, proposed to mercantile leader Joseph Grinnell that they enter into the manufacturing of cotton in the state of Georgia. After surveying the situation, Grinnell suggested instead that the mill be located in New Bedford, feeling the city needed a safe industry for financial investment.

In 1846 Abraham H. Howland procured a charter from the Massachusetts Legislature for a Wamsutta Mills Manufacturing Company of either wool, cotton, or iron to be built in New Bedford. This timely charter was obtained by Grinnell and used to legally start the Wamsutta Mills in 1847 with a small initial capital of $160,000. At first it was difficult to compete with the whaling industry for investment money or employees as the return on textile money, while relatively safe, was low compared to that of the prosperous whaling industry. In spite of these difficulties, land for the first mill on Front Street was bought from Benjamin Rodman for $7,500. The land proved ideal, having a freshwater pond, being in easy reach of the New Bedford and Taunton Railroad, and having access to the railroad wharves. With Joseph Grinnell as president and Thomas Bennett, Jr. as superintendent, Number 1 Mill was built and production began in March of 1849. Wamsutta shirting, the initial product, became the first of many world famous Wamsutta products. Profits were slow but steady, and a second mill was built and in operation in 1855. Two more mills were completed by 1870, following a temporary setback during the Civil War, when southern cotton was all but non-existent. As a result of whalers lost during the Civil War and the Arctic disaster of 1871, the reliable 6% return on the textile stocks looked even more favorable and became the basis for the city's economy. A second textile company, Potomska Mills, opened their doors in the southern section of town in 1871. By 1883 Wamsutta was producing 23,000,000 yards of material, with six mills and a weave shed in full operation employing 26,000 workers. In spite of several strikes, prosperity continued, and a new fabric called "percale" was successfully introduced by Wamsutta Mills in the late 1800s.

Additional textile corporations came to New Bedford, making it a leading center of cotton fabrics in the country. By 1897 there "were twenty five corporations owning fifty mills and running 2,000,000 spindles"[3]. The shift from sea-oriented to land-oriented industries had been successful. Mills had proved to be the mortar which sustained New Bedford's economy during the decline of the Midas like whaling industry.

Other industries contributed to New Bedford's manufacturing economy in the 1800s. Oil was a major part of the city's economy, first through the processing of sperm, whale, fish, and cotton seed oils. Then, following the discovery of petroleum oil, in 1860 New Bedford's son Weston Howland developed a process of refining and marketing the new oil which brought in large profits. Metal works added to the local economy, especially through the success of Stephen A. Morse's company and his development of the twist drill and through the New Bedford Copper Company which merged with the well known Revere Copper Company in 1900. Iron works, brass founderies, machine shops, shoe factories, and many others all added to the growing manufacturing

Typical New Bedford mill

economy. Banks grew and prospered, and money flowed more easily. New Bedford's citizens turned their attentions from the practical to the esthetic and supported such industries as the Mount Washington Glass Company and Pairpoint Manufacturing Company, producers of superior glass and silver artistry, and Charles Taber and Company, early producers of such art specialties as ambrotypes and engravings on glass.

In the late 1800s the massive brick buildings of more than fifty mills stood as commanding structures on the New Bedford skyline and were the centers of her flourishing economy. However, the turn of the century brought ebbs and flows on the economic coastline.

The textile boom rode confidently into the 1900s only to meet economic disaster in the late 1920s. The war effort of World War I initially hurt the mills but soon proved a boon through the need for wartime fabrics. Following the war new products brought new profits, and in 1924 New Bedford's economy appeared to be at an all-time high with employment up and the city at a peak population of 130,000. But it soon proved to be only a shiny veneer as a variety of economic problems slowly began to take their toll.

Many of the mills suffered from poor management, for with

profits high, companies overextended and neglected to reinvest in their facilities. In addition, they made the grave error of lowering the quality of their goods and thus losing their competitive edge over the southern mills which had the advantage of local raw materials and cheaper labor. The market became dangerously over-supplied, prices fell, spindles stood idle, and mills were liquidated. To the already weakened industry came the final blows of severe strikes in 1928 and the national depression in 1929. Except for a few well-managed companies, such as Wamsutta and Berkshire Hathaway Inc., most of the factories closed. Wamsutta held on until 1945 when it was bought out by M. Lowenstein and Sons, leaving Berkshire Hathaway the only one of the "old guard" still producing cloth today.

Following the crash, economic problems plagued the city off and on for the next forty-two years. Factories closed, industries left the city, skilled laborers were attracted elsewhere, unemployment increased, the median number of years of schooling dropped, buildings became vacant and began to deteriorate, and proud historic homes faced neglect and vandalism. To add to these internal problems Massachusetts state taxes, fuel and power costs, unemployment compensation, construction costs, and transportation costs were all higher than in most other states, making it doubly hard to attract new businesses or keep old ones.[4] The Reciprocal Trade Agreements, which allowed imported goods to undersell domestic ones, brought further injury to the few remaining mills. New Bedford was reaching a crisis situation.

Once again New Bedford people took a realistic look at their problems and went to work. Initially they analyzed what attributes New Bedford had and how best to use, develop, restore, and rehabilitate them. The first priority need was for new industry and increased employment. In 1955-1956 the Greater New Bedford Industrial Foundation and the Industrial Development Commission proposed the idea of an industrial park. The development of this privately owned 800-acre Industrial Park, which today supports twenty-two economically viable and diversified companies, first began to turn the tide of New Bedford's economy. It proved to be the first real construction work since the crash of 1929. Secondly, the importance of her seaport was recognized as a major attribute. In 1965-1966 a multi-million dollar hurricane barrier was built, giving New Bedford the unique advantage of a harbor area completely safe from storm damage and flooding. Thirdly, the New Bedford Redevelopment

Fishing fleet (Leonard's Wharf)

Authority was established in the mid 1960s. In an attempt to capitalize on the advantages of the protected harbor, the NBRA developed the North and South Terminal projects along the Acushnet River, which encouraged water related industries. In the South Terminal area existing wharves and piers were rehabilitated, and a 1,665-foot long bulkhead was built. This opened up nineteen acres of new waterfront land, which in turn gave birth to new modern fish processing plants. These plants proved doubly productive, as they increased employment and added to the economy while also having a positive effect on the fishing industry as a whole. To provide greater access to the waterfront area and facilitate the speedy transportation of fresh seafood from New Bedford, the J.F. Kennedy Highway was built in 1975. It runs along the waterfront and connects with Interstate 195.

New Bedford's economic tide has turned, and the sunrise of a new economy is seen on the horizon. Along with the positive effects of the Industrial Park, Hurricane Barrier, and North and South Terminals, textile manufacturing is once again an important part of New Bedford's economic life. Today many of the mills have changed from knitting to needlework. Where factories once made the cloth itself, they now turn ready made fabrics into finished garments with such well-known labels as Kay Windsor, Sharon Jay Togs, Stanley Blacker, and Palm Beach. To further add to the revitalized economy in 1978-1979 the Air Industrial Park, with the special Foreign Trade Zone, was developed. This gives companies a chance to receive, inspect, review, and process merchandise without having to pay customs until the merchandise actually leaves the Foreign Trade Zone — another plus for local industry. New Bedford's economic star has not only begun to rise but is taking its rightful place on the manufacturing horizon of New England.

Today yet another era has come to New Bedford, one which reunites the past with the present — that of tourism and historic preservation. The Waterfront Historic Area LeaguE (WHALE), the Old Dartmouth Historical Society, the Bedford Landing Taxpayers Association, the City of New Bedford, and others have joined forces to restore and rehabilitate historic waterfront areas, homes, commercial buildings, and communities in New Bedford. The city's role has been shaped by pioneering preservationist Mayor John A. Markey, supported by Community Development, the Office of Historic Preservation (the only one in the state), and the Citizens' Advisory Committee. This resurgence has been made possible through the foresighted efforts and monies of her local citizens and historic groups as well as state and federal agencies. Four historic districts have already been designated, with special emphasis on the Waterfront District, where the exteriors of buildings are being restored and interiors are prepared for the practical use of modern day activities.

WHALE and the Office of Historic Preservation, through extensive historic and architectural research, have offered practical guidance for preserving and carefully restoring historic homes throughout the city. Every effort is being made to rehabilitate these structures of historic and architectural value as well as ones that are an integral part of a private or commercial community. In this way communities are being stabilized and their historic, ethnic, and neighborhood values retained while still improving the quality of life. In this positive reuse of existing structures the past is preserved, the present encouraged, and the future enlightened. Here in New Bedford can be found the best of two worlds — a melding of the beauty and significance of history with the practicality of today.

NEW BEDFORD'S PEOPLE

Even though New Bedford's industries have been the mainstay of her economy, it has been her people who have carried her through her successes and trials. Since its inception in 1652, New Bedford has always valued the individual, regardless of religion, color, or ethnic background. While others were turning away so called "different" people, New Bedford welcomed Quakers, Baptists, American Indians, Blacks, West Indians, Cape Verdeans, Azoreans, Madeirans, and Europeans. So that today these varied ancestral bloods, pulsating through the veins of New Bedfordites, provide the strength and character of the city. It is a city where all ethnic groups, though still loyal to their own ancestry, have shared that ancestry and their special talents and aptitudes. Just as many different colors create the beautiful rainbow with its pot of gold, so the different ethnic groups have created New Bedford — a city all its citizens are proud to call home.

Early natives to this area were the Wampanoag Indians. Many of them continued to live as peaceful neighbors to the white settlers, and their descendants can still be found here today. The early settlers were mainly independent Quakers and Baptists who sought freedom of thought and action. As the whaling industry grew, it drew seamen from all nationalities and walks of life. In the late 1700s free Africans began coming to this port as seamen serving on whaling ships. In fact, many harpooners — those who matched their humble human strength and that of an eight foot harpoon against a sixty-five foot, sixty ton whale — were in most cases men of Indian, African, or West Indian descent.

During the early to mid-1700s there were a few slaves held by families in New Bedford, but the basic moral and religious background of the town was strongly against such practices, and by 1785 not a slave was held in the city. As early as 1780 Paul Cuffe, a Black Quaker, and six others petitioned the Colonial government of Massachusetts for the right to vote as taxpayers. In 1783, eighty years before the Civil War, came down the momentous decision that tax paying Blacks had an equal right to vote. Prior to and during the Civil War New Bedford was an active station on the Underground Railroad, helping literally hundreds of slaves to freedom. Here slaves, who had lived in fear and pain, found freedom and a chance for honest industry without the fear of whip or reprisal. For the ways of the Quakers, which at that time were the dominant influence in town, were ones of nonviolence and of social and moral concern for all people. Here a Black man was safe, protected by White and Black alike.

In New Bedford in 1837-1841 Frederick Douglass, who would ultimately lead his people toward final emancipation as· writer, orator, politician, and abolitionist, experienced his first freedom. He was received as a runaway slave and given work at Coffin's Wharf. From here he rose to influence an entire nation and help change an abhorrent way of life to one recognizing universal human rights.

To this center of freedom, where ambitious and industrious men of all backgrounds could seek a better way of life, came people in the early 1800s from Ireland and Portugal and the Portugese Islands of Madeira, the Azores, and Cape Verde (independent since 1975). In the late 1800s people came from France, Canada, Poland, Germany, Russia, Italy, Syria, Spain, Greece, Czechoslovakia, Sweden, Scotland, and Albania. All these ethnic groups brought with them their traditions, cultures, and unique contributions.

The Portugese formed one of the largest ethnic groups in the city, bringing with them a mixture of European, island, and African influence as well as a background strengthened by the Catholic faith and trained in agriculture and the ways of the sea. Many of the Azoreans, Madeirans, and Cape Verdeans came here from islands barely able to supply them with the basic needs of life. They sought a golden opportunity for employment, a chance to develop their talents, establish homes, and provide a better way of life for their families. They earned a reputation for being hard and conscientious workers from the days of whaling through the industrial age up through the present.

When the Portugese first came, they were a foreign group in a strange land with different customs and languages, and they sought strength and comfort among their own. At first they worshiped at St. Mary's Catholic Church, but soon sought a church home of their own where the language and customs were more familiar to them. The faithful were answered in 1871 when the parish of St. John the Baptist, the first Portugese church in the United States, was established under the devoted leadership of Father Joao Ignacio de Azevedo. From this Mother church have come equally devoted and spiritually strong offsprings, who have opened their doors to all of the faithful. However, congregations do tend to draw from similar backgrounds with Our Lady of Assumption serving mainly those from Cape Verde, Mount Carmel those from the Azores, and Immaculate Conception those from Madeira. The Mount Carmel Parish is now the largest in the diocese and celebrated its 75th anniversary in 1979.

In the same vein the Church of the Sacred Heart, built in 1876 on Robeson and Ashland Streets, and St. Hyacinthe Church, built in 1887 on Rivet Street, served the large influx of French Canadians who came to New Bedford to work in the textile mills. The French Canadians, like the Portugese, shared their traditions and talents — thus strengthening New Bedford's cosmopolitan culture.

Along with the Portugese, Cape Verdean, French Canadian, and Black communities came other equally important ethnic groups, such as the Polish, Scandinavian, Greek, and Spanish, all of which have added their special ingredients to this unique community. There are many churches of today which evolved from ethnic contributions, such as: Our Lady of Perpetual Help, Polish; St. Francis of Assisi, Italian; St. Lawrence, Irish; and the French origin churches, St. Anne's, St. Anthony's, and St. Joseph's.

In addition to these contributing ethnic groups there are many special citizens' committees working hand in hand with city officials for the general improvement and progressiveness of this city. Along with these committees the *Standard-Times'* low keyed articles have, in good taste, urged citizens to act to retain their historic treasures. There seems to be a genuine feeling of unity among commerce, government, and private citizens all wanting to make New Bedford the best possible place to live. They care about their city, and they are proud of it. Intangible yes, but these are two of the most important factors in any community. For today there is a noticeable pride in the people toward their city, its history, and its future.

ARCHITECTURE

New Bedford is proud of her rich, architectural heritage, most evident in the variety of her fascinating homes. Herman Melville says it best in *Moby Dick,* in 1861, "The town itself is perhaps the dearest place to live in, in all New England ... nowhere in all America will you find more patrician-like houses; parks and gardens more opulent, than in New Bedford. Whence came they? ... All these brave houses and flowery gardens came from the Atlantic, Pacific, and Indian Oceans. One and all they were harpooned and dragged up hither from the bottom of the sea."[5]

New Bedford's homes follow her history. Days of whaling glory and the rise of the mills are reflected in the beautiful architectural treasures with which the city is so well endowed. The nineteenth century dominates. Little remains of pre-Revolutionary building due to the British invasion of 1778 and prosperity's removal and replacement. The opulent styles of the 1800s — late Federal, Greek Revival, the Gothic Revivals, Italianate, Stick, Queen Anne, Shingle — are perhaps uniquely portrayed in Quaker New Bedford. In the mid-1800s the city was one of the richest per capita in the world, with many astute Quakers being millionaires. They were the prominent builders as well as the economic, political, and moral leaders. However, a wealthy Quaker had a problem, with ostentatious spending frowned upon. The solution is present in the interesting grand houses which remain — tall, straight, and unadorned; and in their simplifying modifications of more elaborate styles. These are in interesting contrast with their more traditional or ornate non-Quaker neighbors of the nineteenth century.

HISTORIC DISTRICTS

The nineteenth century was New Bedford's most magnificent. Whaling kings and industrial giants built their fitting mansions in the interesting styles of the times. These patrician houses were sited in what is now the County Street Historic District. The growth of whaling and industry also required skilled artisans who built their homes in the same architectural styles but on a more modest scale on smaller lots in the present North Bedford Historic District. Meanwhile, the Waterfront Historic District was the commercial center of whaling. Later, with the decline in whaling and the rise of the mills, the financial center moved west, up from the water, to the Central New Bedford Historic District. These distinct neighborhoods remain to provide a guide to the fascinating and complex architecture of the nineteenth century.

IN THE BEGINNING

New Bedford has been exceptional since her earliest settlers came from the Plymouth Colony to brave the wilderness in Dartmouth. The usual Puritan cluster of First Period houses around the meetinghouse was not carried out in New Bedford (then part of Dartmouth.) Here the dissenting Quakers and Baptists chose to dwell on individual homesteads and resented Puritan edicts to be near to and support a meetinghouse. The resulting development of New Bedford was not a direct evolution from a Puritan cluster but a carefully chosen and laid out plan of later whaling barons. This early independence provided the proper background for the ingenious, resourceful, persevering people who created the glorious New Bedford of the late 1700s and 1800s.

ARCHITECTURAL PERIODS OF NEW ENGLAND

The first arrivals did well to build crude shelters, probably a combination of the simplest dwellings remembered from home, the influence of Indian wigwams, and what materials were available. As soon as they could think beyond the huge challenge of pure survival, they began developing their architecture. The first one-room huts were added to or replaced. The two room, central-chimney home gradually evolved into the two story, six to nine room, comfortable Colonial home of the First Period. (to about 1715)

Soon prosperous New England colonists, seeking more opulent surroundings, heard of the British interest in classical architecture in general and the work of the Italian, Andrea Palladio, specifically. Books of his designs arrived and introduced the Palladian or Georgian Period to the colonies. Spacious, symmetrical, with gracious central halls and stairways, elaborate moldings and panelings, and decorative front entries and window treatments, the stylish Georgian Period dominated until about 1785.

The sea, through fortunes reaped from New England whaling, shipbuilding, and world trading, was directly responsible for the Federal Period of Samuel McIntire and Charles Bulfinch. This period followed the Revolution and flowered from about 1785 to about 1820. The immense, delicate, simple elegance of the three-storied Federal home usually featured balustraded low hip roofs, elaborate fences and magnificently detailed porticos and front entries.

Just as the Federal Period was produced from the rewards of the sea, so the rapid rise of intellectual pursuits and later manufacturing and industry mushroomed into the field of architecture. Thomas Jefferson, a major founder of the new Republic, was also a guiding force in her architecture. He led the American interest directly to the cultures and architectures of ancient Rome and Greece. He did not appreciate Georgian and Federal, labeling the former "barbarous" and the latter "pallid," and sought a suitable symbol for the strong democracy of the newly free nation. Greek eventually became the language of democracy and of New England's intellectual awakening, expressed in architecture as well as in literature and art. The resulting Greek Revival Period began about 1820 and remained the most popular choice until about 1850.

Greek temples emerged, most obvious in public buildings where the monumental stone designs were best displayed. The classic temple's features were used with great variety. The portico could extend across the entire front facade or any smaller plan. It could be supported by full-height magnificent columns of a Greek order or small pilasters or anything in between. Greek Revival stressed smooth walls, low-pitched temple roofs, and sharply rectangular windows. If the structure were of wood, it was painted white to remember ancient sun-washed ruins. Most Greek Revival buildings were sited with the gable end facing the street.

The Industrial Revolution sparked the intense changes in architecture which rapidly spiraled from Greek Revival and Gothic Revival to all the Victorian patterns of the 1850s and onward. The nearly overwhelming advances of industry were expressed in the equally nearly overwhelming varieties of architectural styles.

The theme was Revivalism. Revivalism was the outgrowth of

36

the advance in communications, education and the correspon-
ding cultural emphasis, and the technology of the Industrial
Revolution. It was the expression of character — of Victorian
enthusiastic optimism and restless individuality. Fascinating and
confusing, the nineteenth century's styles are a selection from two
thousand years of the world's finest architecture. The features
were often varied and styles combined, giving rise to the Victorian Period's being called "synthetic eclecticism." The chart on
the pages following this section graphically displays the styles,
gives a brief description of features often associated with each,
and lists illustrative New Bedford buildings.

New Bedford's architecture is as unique as the city, which is
actually a museum of one of the richest Victorian heritages in
New England. Many of the splendid homes of her whaling captains and merchants and impressive mansions of her mill kings
have been preserved. The interesting Quaker influence is most
obvious in New Bedford. Her far-sighted present preservation efforts provide a rich heritage to study and appreciate. The unique
living history of her working historic waterfront is available for all
to enjoy. Like Boston, New Bedford is a city of interesting and
distinct neighborhoods ready to be explored.

GLOSSARY OF HELPFUL TERMS

balustrade — a handrail or low parapet supported by short
pillars called balusters

bargeboard — a board attached to the edge of a gable roof,
usually ornately carved

belvedere — summerhouse or open, roofed gallery with a view,
often placed on roof tops in New Bedford

brackets — braces, often ornamental and at roof line

cornice — the top horizontal part of an entablature (atop a column) or projecting from on top of a wall

entablature — the horizontal parts surmounting columns or
pilasters

gable — or pediment, triangular end of building, formed by
slopes of pitched roof

gambrel roof — roof with two slopes, the lower slope is the
steeper

hip roof — roof with four slopes which meet at the center thus
forming four angles

lantern — open or windowed structure on top of roof

lintel — horizontal top part of window or door opening

mansard roof — roof with two slopes on all four sides, lower slope is almost vertical and upper almost horizontal

order — a classical system with column and entablature

Palladian window — in Georgian and later Stick Style, a featured, large, arched window, usually over front entry

pediment — the triangular, crowning feature of porticos, doorways, windows

pilaster — a flat form of a column applied to a wall

portico — covered colonnade at the entrance of a building

quoins — decorative feature of squared stones, with long and short faces alternately displayed, at corner of buildings

string courses — brick or stone course in horizontal line of emphasis under windows, or separating floors

tracery — ornamental stone work carved in patterns in Gothic windows

vergeboards — see bargeboards

A FIELD GUIDE TO IDENTIFYING AND RECOGNIZING ARCHITECTURAL PERIODS AND STYLES WITH FOCUS ON NEW BEDFORD ARCHITECTURE

Period or Style:
Federal Period or
Adam Style
1785-1820

Features:
Low pitched roof, immense, simple, delicate, elegant, three story square, balustraded roof and fence, magnificent front entry

Location:
*Mariners' Home
*Samuel Rodman, Jr. House
*Rodman Candleworks
*Standish House
*Benjamin Rodman House
  (NB Glass Museum)
*Francis Rotch House
*David Coffin House
*Henry Beetle House
*Sundial Building
  (Commercial)
*William Tallman Warehouse

*see index for further information

Late Federal, Greek Rev.:
*Jireh Perry (Masonic)
*Charles Russell House
*Andrew Robeson House
*George Howland, Jr.
*First Baptist Church

Period or Style:
Greek Revival
1820-1860 forerunner
of classical styles

Features:
Gable facing street, massive portico with Greek order columns or pilasters, smooth walls, low pitch roof, sharp rectangular windows, white or stone, Ionic pilasters with recessed panels on corners of buildings

Location:
*US Custom House
*Double Bank Building
*William Rotch, Jr
*Capt. Henry Taber
*William Tallman Russell
*Joseph Grinnell Mansion
*William R. Rodman Mansion
*Haile Luther House
*John Avery Parker
 89 Hawthorne Street
 34 Sixth Street
*Friends Meeting House

Period or Style:
Early Gothic
Revival
Picturesque Gothic
Gothic Cottage
1820s-1870s

Features:
Tall, steep, pointed arch dominates, pinnacles, battlements, window tracery, gingerbread bargeboards, veranda, one color

Location:
*Wm. J. Rotch Gothic Cot.
*Unitarian Church
*Samuel W. Rodman House
 27 Maple Street
 36 Grove Street

Later Gothic Revival:
*Thomas H. Knowles
*George Howland, Jr. Carriage House

Period or Style:
Italian Villa Style
1837-1870

Features:
Asymmetrical, with square tower, lantern, or cupola, off centered, projected bracketed cornices, arched windows, grouped bays, balustraded balconies, verandas; in New Bedford second only to Queen Anne in popularity

Location:
*Jireh Swift, Jr. House
*Edward S. Taber House
*Union Street Houses
148 Hawthorne Street
603 County Street
465 County Street
96 Madison Street
397 County Street

Period or Style:
Octagon Mode
1848-1860

Features:
Octagon, two to four stories, low roof, capped by belvedere

Location:
*The Octagon

Period or Style:
High Victorian
Gothic
1860s-1890s

Features:
Early Gothic with at least two colors or kinds of materials (stone) combined, heavy molding & carved detail, appears heavy, solid, windows set in, complex roof lines, heavy spires & towers, mostly

40   *see index for further information

masonry for public buildings; goal: reality, forceful character, not beauty alone

Location:
*Grace Episcopal Church

Period or Style:
High Victorian
Italianate
1860s-1890s

Features:
Has obvious projecting, bracketed cornice of Italian Villa Style plus: variety of lines in arched windows, large brackets, crowded facade, moldings, ornaments, varied windows; goal: strong character, self made, democratic

Location:
139 Cottage Street
179 Cottage Street

Period or Style:
Second Empire Style
1860s-1890s
French High
Victorian

Features;
French, always has high mansard roof enveloping entire floor, dormers, detailed chimneys, projecting pavilions, tall, bold, appears three dimensional, similar to Italianate

Location:
*Gilbert Russell House
*James Arnold Mansion
*Thomas Lothrop (K. of C.)
 91 State Street
 144 Summer Street

Period or Style:
Stick Style
1850s-1880s

Features:
Tall, with high pitched roof; complex; rectangularly irregular projected eaves with large brackets; exposed framing in

gable end; verandas with posts with diagonal braces; bisected triangle & diagonal stick work; exterior boards have overlay — vertical, horizontal, diagonal — like sticks to suggest structure, exposed cross bracing; one of few purely American styles of 19th century; goal: truthful character cultivation

Location:
27 Seventh Street
97 Madison Street
591 County Street
398 County Street

Period or Style:
Queen Anne Style
1870s-1890s

Features:
Irregular plan and massing, varied color & texture, projections, window variety, bays, high multiple roof, turrets, chimneys emphasized, small classical detail, carving; most popular New Bedford style; considered practical rather than philosophical

Location:
*Joseph A. Beauvais
*Andrew G. Pierce, Jr.
 691 County Street
 140 Cottage Street
 154 Cottage Street
 347 Pleasant Street
 151 Summer Street
 413 County Street

Period or Style:
Shingle Style
1880s-1890s

Features:
Shingles on most walls, even posts of verandas, or stone on ground floor, bands of windows plus one Palladian, gambrel roof, hip or gable or both, simpler & quieter than Queen Anne & more organized, mass appears to bulge,

*see index for further information

reverse of Stick Style: hides all framework and inner structure, often includes Queen Anne features, one of few American designs, began in New England

Location:
*Benjamin Anthony

Period or Style:
Richardsonian
Romanesque
1885-1910

Features:
America's famous son, architect Henry Hobson Richardson; varied materials & colors, usually stone, huge, round, Romanesque arch, often combine rectangular & arched windows, with a ribbon of each per story, arched windows with separating colonnettes, capped turrets, heavy chimneys; effect: single bulging mass

Location:
Pilgrim United Church of Christ
Former Citizen National Bank, corner Second & William Streets

GUIDED TOUR OF NEW BEDFORD

DIRECTIONS: New Bedford is easily reached from Route 195, Route 140, or Route 6. From Route 195 take Exit 15, following the "Downtown" signs. As you near the city from all routes, signs for "Downtown" and the "Moby Dick Trail" will guide you to the Whaling Museum and the heart of the city where the tour begins. There are two centrally located parking areas, one on William Street at Second Street and the other at the foot of Second Street on Elm Street.

WATERFRONT HISTORIC DISTRICT
NRHP, National Landmark District

The waterfront has been an important center since New Bedford's early days. This capital of the romantic whaling industry still largely depends on her working waterfront. The narrow, cut stone streets, cobblestone and brick walks, lighted by replicas from the past, invite you to explore — to see not only what a whaling port was but what an active, successful seaport is today. The Waterfront Historic District is best enjoyed on foot as the atmosphere and architectural detail become a blur through a car window.

In 1765 Joseph Rotch purchased his ten acres (part of the present Waterfront Historic District) in and around which all of New Bedford was to develop. Within ten years of Rotch's purchase, New Bedford was the second largest whaling port in New England. The land was further sub-divided, streets expanded, and the Waterfront District was alive with the sights and sounds of all the activities whaling involved. The British Invasion in 1778 snuffed out this life of whaling which didn't recover until after 1785. The War of 1812 halted the advancing whaling industry, but not for long. By 1830 New Bedford had become the largest American whaling center. The Waterfront District teemed with activity of wharves, countinghouses, taverns, smithies, rope

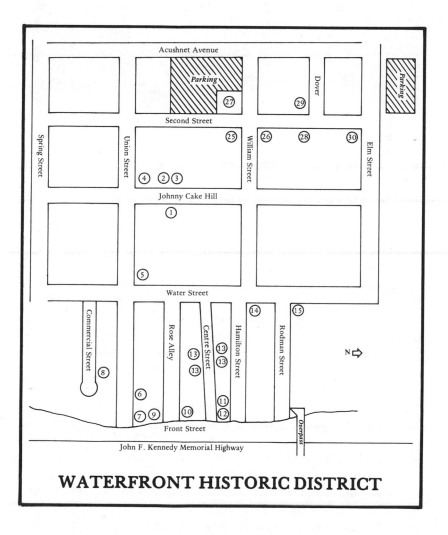

WATERFRONT HISTORIC DISTRICT

New Bedford Waterfront, 1978

makers, riggers, and candle makers. The mid-1800s marked the height of whaling which had noticeably declined by 1870. Success was expressed in Greek Revival and in the important buildings designed in that intellectually-valued classical style.

The prosperity of the whaling days is still evident here. You expect to see Herman Melville wandering the streets of his New Bedford which he described in *Moby Dick*, written in 1861. Melville's opulent picture became tarnished with the decline of whaling and the Waterfront District deteriorated to being called a "wino jungle," a description gleaned from the combination of overgrowth of ailanthus and waterfront unfortunates.

In the 1960s concerned citizens and government agencies studied the problem, and the 1970s saw the results of Herculean effort. Mayor John A. Markey and many city, state, and federal agencies joined private interests led by WHALE* (Waterfront Historic Area LeaguE) in a unique cooperative to achieve the amazing revitalization of the district.

Even in the heart of the tourist season you're very likely to be greeted by a passerby with a quick, friendly word of welcome — a sign of civic interest, showing New Bedford to be a proud city that cares. You're invited to wander and explore and share the New Bedford experience.

Whaling Museum

#1

The Whaling Museum	To reach the Whaling Museum
Old Dartmouth Historical	from either parking lot, return to
Society	Second and William Streets, walk
1904, 1916, 1935, 1972,	one block toward the water, turn
1979	right on Johnny Cake Hill, and
Open all year, fee charged	the museum is on the left.

The saga of the whale and the men dedicated to hunting it comes alive at the Whaling Museum in this, the whale industry's greatest port. Here you can board the *Lagoda*, the largest ship model in the world, and relive the days when whaling was king.

The whaler's fishing grounds were the whole world. Here at the museum are displayed treasures of the Orient, fine silver, china, crystal, and pewter, as well as paintings of gallant ships and their captains. All of these attest to the riches of these world travelers.

The long voyage of a whale ship, often three or four years, produced a life of its own. This life is reflected in the collections of the true American folk art of scrimshaw, intricate carvings, and paintings depicting whaling adventures and life in remote parts of the world. Completing the picture are displays of

Whaling Museum **Lagoda**

figureheads, sternboards, ship models, and fascinating logbooks containing factual accounts, sketches, and humor.

The *Lagoda,* a half-scale, accurate replica of a square rigged whaler, is the main feature of the central Bourne Building. The perfect detail of the model adds to the fun of climbing aboard and exploring. It provides an exact background in which to relive the days of whaling. The suspended skeleton of a small humpback whale fits the scale of the *Lagoda.* Nearby, a fully and meticulously rigged whaleboat, made of cedar and approximately thirty feet long, looks as if it had just been lowered from the davits of a whale ship and is ready to row or sail closer to the sighted whale. These exhibits, plus those of other whaling gear, provide strong visual appeal.

Portions of the unbelievably immense Purrington and Russell panorama are specially displayed. The panorama depicts a world-wide whaling voyage and measures eight and a half feet tall and 1275 feet, more than a quarter of a mile, long. Scenes show sightings, chase, capture, return, blubber stripping, trying, disasters, and successes of a whaling adventure. Another portion is a view of Tahiti as seen by whalemen when calling for provisions and water.

The supporting industries of whaling are viewable in a series of separate room displays — of a chandlery, tin and copper shop, blockmaker, cooperage, and countinghouse. "The Window on Centre Street," offers a view of present day Centre Street which also reflects the past. For you can look out with bankers, lawyers, insurance men and others whose offices here in the 1800s enabled them to watch the activity of the waterfront and their fortunes being made.

The museum collection has increased, and buildings have been added over the years. At the turn of the twentieth century Old Dartmouth Historical Society and museum were established. The tiny collection was displayed in the Society's rooms in the old Masonic Building at Pleasant and Union Streets. By 1907 the collection had outgrown its setting and was moved to its permanent quarters in the Bank of Commerce building on Water Street. This was the first building in the present six-building museum complex. This first building is now named the Rogers Building in honor of its donor, Henry Huttleston Rogers, noted benefactor of neighboring Fairhaven.

In 1916 the large, central building and half-scale ship model were given by Miss Emily Howland Bourne in memory of her father, Jonathan Bourne*. (See Bourne Counting House.)

Bourne was a most successful whaling merchant, owner of more whaling ships than anyone else in New England, and an industrial giant.

Appropriately named, the Bourne Building houses the model of Bourne's favorite ship, the bark *Lagoda*. Merchant ships in those days were often named to honor the countries with which they would trade. The *Lagoda* was named after a Russian lake called Ladoga, but the builder reversed the letters, and the error was perpetuated, possibly for the thrifty Yankee reason that her registration fee had been paid under that name.

In 1977 an awe inspiring sight greeted those first to arrive here after the nearby explosion and fire which destroyed buildings along Union Street and severely damaged the Sundial Building*. The *Lagoda* appeared to be undersail with sails billowing from the explosion — seemingly in an effort to leave the scene at full sail!

The Bourne Building, designed after the Georgian Custom House in Salem, is of brick laid in Flemish bond. The arched windows are particularly notable, with quoins of stone at the corners of the building. The interesting doors and windows are highlighted, and the denticulated roof line is crowned by a small observatory and whale weathervane.

The site of the Bourne Building was carefully chosen. It was not only close to the Rogers Building, it was the scene of early brothels, sailors' taprooms, and other frowned-upon associations. It was felt that the museum would be more in keeping with the goals of the Bethel across the street, in an effort to improve the moral values of seamen.

The Bourne Building faces Johnny Cake Hill, believed to be the site of ancient Indian burial grounds. It was first called "Journey Cake Hill" by early Quakers as the place where they stopped briefly to eat their corn meal journey cakes on the way to and from meeting. The name was changed to Johnny Cake to honor a favorite political leader, Jonathan Trumbell.

In 1935 the Wood Building was added to the museum complex and named in honor of the museum's first curator and his wife. The Museum Theater was added in 1972 and a new building to house the library in 1979. The separate buildings are so harmoniously unified it is hard to distinguish the individual structures. The proud Georgian Revival Bourne Building is central. The Rogers, Hirst, and Wood Buildings, plus the modern Theater Building, fit perfectly, continuing the flow of brick in a current manner. The landscaping and formal gardens provide further peaceful unity.

The museum offers informative daily walking tours in season, a movie, and many other educational experiences. This museum of New Bedford history is actually a view into world history. For, as you lose yourself in its interesting, well displayed exhibits, following the paths of early whalers, you circumnavigate the globe.

Seamen's Bethel

#2
Seamen's Bethel
15 Johnny Cake Hill
1832
Open every weekend,
  daily in season, &
  special occasions,
  no fee.

Across the street from The Whaling Museum stands the Seamen's Bethel.

"Enter to rest, to meditate, to pray."⁴ Enter and sit where captains and sailors have been sitting for decades. Face the pulpit in the shape of a bowsprit, a familiar sight to seamen easily translated into a symbolic ship of faith to carry them safely over raging seas and endless horizons. To the Bethel have come

51

seamen from all over the world with a hundred different backgrounds, each in his own way seeking an inner strength and faith. Out from these doors has gone a lasting influence that in time has touched men in every port and on every ocean.

All about you speaks of the sea — from the three-masted whaling schooner sitting high atop the Bethel, symbolic of the many whalemen who entered these doors during the 1800s to prepare themselves for voyages lasting three to four years, down to the very cushions on the pews made of sail canvas. One such pew was occasionally occupied by Herman Melville. Notice the cenotaphs on the walls, each in memory of one or two or in some cases whole crews who lost their lives at sea. The youngest was only eighteen and the oldest forty-nine. These plaques speak eloquently of the dangerous everyday life of a seaman. You can better understand why Herman Melville wrote in his classic *Moby Dick,* "...there stands a Whaleman's Chapel, and few are the moody fishermen, shortly bound for the Indian Ocean or Pacific, who fail to make a Sunday visit to the spot."[7]

Visit the vestry directly below the chapel. This room, better known as the "Old Salt Box," was named for the hold of a ship where fish were stored and preserved in salt. The preserving of fish is symbolic of the preserving of men's souls. Here seamen met for education as well as inspiration.

Why was the Bethel founded? In the early 1800s all levels of society existed in New Bedford — from the socially elite, living off the monies of their successes, through the many levels of a working society, down to the derelicts, harlots, thieves, and murderers, people living in the depth of despair and degradation. These cast offs of society lived in certain sections of town, which were carefully avoided by respectable citizens. They seemed to exist outside the law.

In the late 1820s, following the murder of a ship's carpenter, a group of citizens took matters into their own hands. At that time there was an old whaler, called the *Ark,* which had been converted into an especially unsavory brothel. It was tied up near the foot of Water Street. This band of citizens converged on the *Ark,* burning it to the water's edge. In retaliation a waterfront mob burned the Elm Street Methodist Church. Once again the citizens took the law into their own hands and burned *Ark II,* which had been made from the hull of another whaler and was even worse than the first *Ark.* Finally on June 30, 1830, in order to stop this useless rioting and retaliating, a group of men instituted a Committee of Vigilance. Among these men were

Bow shaped pulpit and interior of Seamen's Bethel

Samuel and Benjamin Rodman, Seth Russell, Joseph Ricketson, John Howland, Jr., and Nathan Hathaway. Slowly tempers cooled and reason prevailed.

Still into this port came 5,000 sailors annually. In an attempt to further counteract the ills of society, a group of local businessmen, headed by Samuel Rodman, Jr., founded the New Bedford Port Society in 1830. Its purpose was stated: "for the moral improvement of seamen, and the furnishing of material relief to needy seamen and their families."[8] It proved to be a practical answer to a difficult situation. From the time the Bethel opened on May 2, 1832, this non-denominational, on-going Christian service has counseled and supported seamen and their families. Weddings and funerals have been performed, and thanksgiving, memorial, and Sunday services held at the chapel, in homes, and on the waterfront. Thousands of Bibles and New Testaments have been placed aboard ships. During the whaling era the chapel also served as an invaluable source of contact by listing the crews of every ship sailing from New Bedford.

The Bethel has had its humorous moments as well as its serious ones. Prior to the fire in 1866, the pulpit was on the street side of the chapel. To facilitate late arrivals, when the church was renovated, the entire seating arrangement was reversed, putting the pulpit where it is today. Being victims of habit, when the congregation stood for hymns and scripture readings, they still turned to face the street side, backs to the pulpit. This was effectively remedied when a visiting preacher, feeling the congregation was being impolite to him, stood and gave his entire sermon with his back to the congregation. Needless to say, he got his point across.

On the downhill side of the chapel is the recently completed Memorial Garden dedicated to all the chaplains of the Seamen's Bethel. It was appropriately dedicated on the two hundredth anniversary of the birth of the Bethel's first chaplain, the Reverend Enoch Mudge. The gardens were designed by Lucia Kerr Paull to provide a background for weddings and an area for rest and meditation. Notice the exposed rock ledge, symbolizing the firm foundation of a church built on a rock.

This simple, grey clapboard building, without fanfare or fancy ecclesiastical trappings, has inspired a world.

#3
Mariners' Home   Next door to the Bethel is the
Johnny Cake Hill   **Mariners' Home.**
c1790
Not open to public.

Next to the Bethel stands the Mariners' Home, a haven for transient seamen. Since the Home opened in 1857, any seaman having been at sea within six months has been welcomed. For a nominal fee he receives a clean bed, good food, and a friendly understanding ear in a wholesome atmosphere. Here too a sailor can obtain reliable information concerning which ships are in port and might need additional crew members.

This restored Federal mansion was built circa 1790 on the corner of William and North Water Streets. It was the home of William Rotch, Jr., uncle of Samuel Rodman, Jr., prime organizer and first president of the New Bedford Port Society. In 1850 Rotch's daughter, Sarah Arnold, deeded the mansion to the Port Society as a home for sailors, and her husband, James Arnold, financed the move to its present location. Arnold was an early president of the New Bedford Port Society and Sarah the first president of the ladies' branch of the Society.

This three story, grey clapboard and brick Federal, built

Mariers' Home

near the end of the Revolutionary War, is one of the few to remain from that period. It originally rested on the foundation of the home of Joseph Rotch, William's grandfather and New Bedford's early dominant leader of its whaling industry.

#4
Eggers Building
1 Johnny Cake Hill
c1872
Open as business

Walk south down Johnny Cake Hill, past the Bethel, to the NW corner of Union Street. On the right is the Eggers Building and small complex of shops.

The Eggers Building, a venacular Greek Revival facing Union Street, is part of an eye-appealing, small complex of shops. The successful adaptive rehabilitation work, a combination of public and private efforts, completely replaces what was once the scene of destruction.

In 1977 an explosion and fire destroyed the Union Tobacco building on this site, plus two others across Johnny Cake Hill on Union Street, and caused some damage on William Street. Sadly, one of the Union Street buildings, the Macomber-Sylvia, had just been restored by WHALE*. Almost immediately plans emerged to move the Eggers Building, then on William Street, to this location. The restored Eggers Building is an integral part of the complex, which includes a modern concrete and brick addition and a new frame and shingle structure combined harmoniously. An ancient well, featured in an old New Bedford painting in the Whaling Museum, was found during the work, though recovered for safety. The building derives its name from George Eggers, a talented gunsmith and whalecraft manufacturer.

#5
Sundial Building
Union and Water Streets
c1820
HABS

Walk down Union Street toward the water. The first building on the left, at the NW corner of Union and Water Streets, is the Sundial Building.

Built about 1820 and within ten years known as the "Sundial Building," the structure was named for the interesting sundial above the Union Street entrance. Here clocks and chronometers were manufactured. The dial's time was referred to as "New Bedford time" by seamen and used to set nautical instruments and chronometers by New Bedford sailors throughout the world. The clock accurately tells standard time to this day.

A 1977 explosion and fire almost totally destroyed the Sundial Building, which has been called the sixth best building in the Waterfront District. Within days WHALE* acquired the wreck and stabilized its unsafe condition. Mayor Markey pledged Community Development funds, the Massachusetts Historical Commission pledged Heritage Conservation and Recreation Service funds, and, with WHALE and private individuals funding the remainder, restoration began. This immediate joint action rescued and restored the treasure.

The Sundial Building was constructed of brick and stone in the late Federal style about 1820 by Charles* and Seth Russell, Jr*. The land had been sold to their father by his uncle, New Bedford founder Joseph Russell III. A West India goods store previously occupied the site before the Russells' Sundial Building was built to house their dry goods store. The second floor had offices of lawyers and a sheriff, and the top floor contained a sailor's room, library, and museum. In 1850 the *Evening Standard* began publication here, and the first plate glass window in New Bedford was installed. This once prestigious location of elite shops and businesses has been used for a variety of interesting purposes: clockmaker shop, nautical instrument sales, observatory, hotel, textile lab, and a fruit company.

In 1823 and 1828 the Sundial Building was mortgaged for $4,000; in 1828 Charles Russell was offered $8,851 as a loan against it; in 1845 it sold for $10,525; in 1942 it sold for $4,000; and in 1978 it was estimated at $320,000 to totally rehabilitate.

The adjacent garden was designed and installed by the Buzzards Bay Garden Club, aided by the Old Dartmouth Historical Society* and WHALE*. This small area of quiet incorporated the fieldstone and brick foundations of buildings lost in the 1977 fire into an attractive backdrop for the plantings.

#6

Benjamin Taber Building
31 Union Street
Possibly open as business

Continue east down Union on the same side of the street. The Benjamin Taber Building is the second building up from the corner of Union and Front Streets.

Preservation efforts hope to rescue this ancient sailors' boardinghouse and adapt it for commercial, office, and living use in keeping with the area. It was once believed by some to be the famous Spouter's Inn of *Moby Dick.* Careful research revealed that though seamen did board here, it was not the inn of Melville's description.

First built by Benjamin Taber for his son, in 1798 it was the home of a marine captain and his wife, who remained here until 1834. Then the second and third floors were a sailors' boarding house until 1925. The ground floor, which was probably added about 1828 by raising the other stories, housed stores — produce and fish markets until 1910, followed by a meat provisioner, later a fish processing house.

#7

Seth Russell, Sr. House
Union and Front Streets
c1765
Open as business

The next building, at the NW corner of Union and Front Streets, is the Seth Russell, Sr. House.

It is believed that Seth Russell, Sr. built this house in 1765, though the date is presently being researched. If so, it now remains one of the rare structures in the city to pre-date the Revolution. Why it was spared the British torch in the 1778 invasion is a question.

Some say it was chance that the British merely sought to cripple the privateers and any related land support and were not interested in destroying houses. Some say the owner was a Tory and his British friends aided him by saving the house. A third theory believes the owner was such a Patriot that the revenge-seeking British figured sparing the house would cast suspicion upon him.

The original owner, Seth Russell, Sr., was the nephew of the founder of New Bedford, Joseph Russell III. This Quaker family, Seth and sons Seth, Jr. and Charles, were prominent in whaling and other mercantile concerns. They owned the bark *Catherine,* which was captured in the War of 1812. Their business interests were wide, and their land holdings grew until most were lost as a result of the financial crash of the 1830s.

The house itself was situated on Water Street for centuries until its move to Union and Front Streets, where it was partially restored. Removing it from its former location provided expansion space for the Whaling Museum's new library. Though possibly constructed prior to the Revolution, the building has been modified considerably and is generally a Greek Revival style. No longer a private home, the structure has seen many uses: insurance and law offices, a hat and cap company, a tailor shop, coal and wood office, tin smith, boardinghouse, and a marine electronics supply company.

#8

C. E. Beckman Co.
35 Commercial Street
c1842 main building,
    c1790s wooden building
Open as marine supply
    business

For a slight detour around the block, return on Union Street to Water Street. Turn left and left again on Commercial Street to the C. E. Beckman Co.

The main building was constructed as a store about 1842 by Gideon Howland. The older wooden building was used for the storage of whale oil. Both buildings have been closely tied with the sea. Here were housed a countinghouse, sail loft, ship and sign painters, riggers, and offices over the years. In 1885 a ships' chandlery was opened. The whale outfitters expanded, and the company continues today as a modern marine supply business.

#9

John Tabor Building
Front Street and Rose Alley
c1820
Private
HABS

Return to the corner of Union and Front Streets. Walk north a short block to Rose Alley, where roses once lined the lane, home to workers tied to the sea. Nearby an old well, called Aqua Rosa Pumpa, reportedly produced such sweet water it was specified in local recipes. At the corner is the John Tabor Building.

This three story granite ashlar building is nearly covered with vines. A very solid structure, the second and third floors are suspended from large trusses by wrought iron rods.

#10

McCullough Building
Front Street
circa early 1800s
Open as shop

Continue north on Front Street. The next building on the left is the McCullough Building.

Not long ago this stylish building was known as the McCullough Ruin, as only the two side, foot-thick, stone walls were standing. Another preservation achievement, it now houses a shop with offices and a loft apartment.

An early owner, an Irishman named McCullough, arrived here in 1847 destined to become the first foreign born citizen elected to office in New Bedford. McCullough was a supplier to whalemen, a salvage operator and dealer. From his successful operations he fitted whale ships and lived in a splendid house elsewhere in the city.

#11

William Tallman
Warehouse
Front and Centre Streets
c1790
Open as businesses
HABS

Continue on Front Street to Centre Street with the William Tallman Warehouse, which houses WHALE, on the north corner.

Once Centre Street was lined with commercial buildings on both sides, with whaling trypots at the foot of the street. Now on

William Tallman Warehouse

Centre Street only the Tallman Warehouse pre-dates the War of 1812 and is one of the oldest buildings to survive in New Bedford. It was originally built about 1790 as a store and warehouse by William Tallman on land purchased from Joseph Russell III, New Bedford's founder.

Whaling pioneers Tallman and Joseph III and Caleb Russell jointly owned four small whaling sloops as early as 1765. William Tallman later shifted his interests from whaling to general merchandizing during the Revolution. At that time Tallman, a Quaker, was a commissary of subsistence for the Patriots. The 1778 British raid destroyed his goods in Bedford Village, took him prisoner, and confiscated his knee buckles, shoe buckles, and his favorite horse. His liberty, horse, and buckles were returned at the order of the British general. He continued his leading role in New Bedford as a selectman on the first board of selectmen from the 1787 incorporation until his death in 1802.

The warehouse was constructed in the Federal commercial style. The random stone walls are dressed with small, closely laid painted bricks. The structure is two attached buildings, separated at the roof line and by their different colors. On Front Street the central hoist on the top floor can be seen.

The Tallman Warehouse is typical of the whaling days of New Bedford. In 1820 the fire, which destroyed most of the

Centre Street buildings, damaged the warehouse, then a grocery. It has since housed a ship chandlery, iron trade business, shops, offices, and a warehouse and cold storage plant. Its adaptive reuse as the office of WHALE*, a marine financial office, an apartment on the top floor, and a chandlery on the west half is characteristic of the Waterfront Historic District today.

#12

Waterfront Historic Area LeaguE (WHALE) 13 Centre Street Open all year, no fee	WHALE is housed in the William Tallman Warehouse on the north corner of Centre and Front Streets.

WHALE, formed in the early 1960s, is a non-profit organization of private citizens interested in reviving and preserving the waterfront area. At its formation, WHALE recalled the glorious, exciting, flourishing times of the waterfront area in the 1840s, looked at the then present waterfront's degradation and deterioration, and decided to do something about it.

From 1963 to 1965 they made a detailed study of the waterfront and, when renewal plans stalled, pushed for Historic District classification to prevent further destruction. Through their revolving fund WHALE began buying properties to protect them from permanent loss. Through the National Trust for Historic Preservation, in 1975 WHALE began a preservation and design service providing architectural advice and working drawings to guide preservation work. This helped neighbors do their own rehabilitation work. Successful progress could be attributed to WHALE's goal of adaptive preservation, to saving historically important structures and using them in modern, productive ways, and to their working in close cooperation with government agencies.

In the 1970s the dream became a reality with the cooperative linking of three major groups in the district into the Ten Acre Revival, and the arrival of John K. Bullard, the agent for these three divergent groups. Bullard recognized and understood their varying compositions and interests. Through communication, recognition of the importance of each, and stressing their common goals, the resulting cooperative unity has accomplished the thriving, presently useful, historically fascinating Waterfront District you see today. The three groups are the Old Dartmouth Historical Society, responsible for the

Whaling Museum; WHALE; and the Bedford Landing Tax-payers Association, representing the district's business people.

The successful philosophy of Bullard's, in recognizing and stressing the sense of community among the people, results in all cooperating to achieve their universal goals and still being able to react and adapt as the situation requires. He aims for a true neighborhood evolution which retains the character and allows free choice. Success has been staggering.

WHALE has been a vital agent for positive change in the rescue and rehabilitation of the Rodman Candleworks, Benjamin Rodman House (New Bedford Glass Museum), Pairpoint Glassworks, Andrew Robeson House, Haile Luther House, Spooner and Beetle Houses, Tallman Warehouse, Seth Russell House, William Tallman Russell House, and the Sundial Building, all of which have separate references in this text. Individual preservation achievements are tied together within the Waterfront Historic District by the city-provided: special paving-block streets, cobblestone and brick walks, and period lighting, plus replica street signs made by vocational high school students.

WHALE also acts as needed to encourage other groups whose interests benefit New Bedford. They were instrumental in backing the New Bedford Glass Society and in encouraging Pair-point Glassworks to return to New Bedford. WHALE housed the Glass Society in their own offices until their joint efforts saw the Benjamin Rodman House restored and become the New Bedford Glass Museum. WHALE provided the Bourne Warehouse for the Glassworks and moved the gigantic Andrew Robeson House to make way for needed new glass furnaces which enabled the Pair-point Glassworks to return. WHALE has worked to secure the headquarters of the *Ernestina,* the immigration packet which sailed between the Cape Verde Islands and New Bedford. WHALE has supported the Public Arts Council in their goal to make all the arts available to the public.

WHALE physically extended beyond the Waterfront Historic District when they purchased the Hatch properties to save that visible historical neighborhood and draw the line against erosion. The Hatch houses are examples of nineteenth century venacular homes, close to downtown and across from the harbor, on Pleasant Street bounded by Hillman and Maxfield Streets. Architectural styles range from modified Federal to Greek Revival, Victorian, Italianate, and Gothic Cottage. WHALE has restored the structures for resale and adaptive reuse here in the North Bedford Historic District.

62

The improved physical environment and resulting commercial vitality provide a Waterfront Historic District which attracts visitors and at the same time supports flourishing, vital fishing and related businesses. This success is the achievement of the people of New Bedford who, with pride and a sense of history, had the foresight to preserve their past and adapt it for their present and future.

#13
Centre Street

The following buildings are found along Centre Street: Caleb Spooner House, 22 Centre Street, 1806, shop open; Henry Beetle House, 24 Centre Street, 1804, private; John Harrison Building, 23 Centre Street, c1820, open as business, HABS; William Maxfield Building, 25 Centre Street, c1821 & 1854, open as business.

Historically important and presently significant, Centre Street is directly opposite the working waterfront, in the shadow of modern freighters, scallopers, and draggers. The move and restoration of the Spooner and Beetle Houses have triggered the revitalization of Centre Street which was nearly totally destroyed during the 1778 British Invasion, again by fire in 1820, and more recently by neglect.

The tidy, restored **Caleb Spooner House,** typical of New Bedford in the early 1800s, was moved here to save it from its West End demolition site. WHALE partially restored it and sold it to Allen and Mary Scott who completed its rehabilitation. The Scotts, in turn, organized the now annual Centre Street Festival* which draws the interest of residents and visitors to appreciate the Centre Street revival.

In 1806 Caleb Spooner, a brick layer, built this Cape style home for his bride after their wedding in the First Congregational Church, now Unitarian. The seven rooms had many fireplaces, the wide stairway was enclosed, and hand-hewn roof beams were secured with huge wooden pegs. Caleb's father was a farmer and a Minuteman who marched from Dartmouth to Lexington in April of 1775. The house remained in the Spooner family for nearly a century.

Early Centre Street

Centre Street (today)

Three generations of spar makers in the Beetle family have been housed in the Federal period **Henry Beetle House** next door. It was also home to Thomas Thompson, called the "man in overalls" mayor of New Bedford. "Tom" Thompson came up through the Wamsutta Mills where he began working at the age of eleven when financial necessity ended his formal education. A

Caleb Spooner House and Henry Beetle House

self educated man of many interests, he was a ballplayer, violin player, avid reader, and by 1906 an accomplished marble cutter by trade. His marble shop became a drawing center for a variety of people who discussed a variety of topics. Thompson, always leader of this forum, was a lively, quick-thinking speaker, a great stump speaker who published his own paper with his forum's views. As the twenty-first mayor, his goal was to benefit people.

A fine example of a commercial building, recognized by HABS, is the **John Harrison Building,** across Centre Street at number 23. Four stories tall, it was built soon after the fire in 1820 of granite rubble faced with brick. It served as a wholesale beef provisioner, contained offices in the late 1800s, was an ice plant in the early 1900s, and now houses a beef wholesaler.

The **William Maxfield Building** at 25 Centre Street was actually two separate, now attached, structures. Part was built shortly after 1820 and the rest about 1854. The sign, appropriate here where the 1854 occupant was a ship painter, was designed by Frank H. Purrington and has been here since 1900.

Double Bank Building

#14

Double Bank Building	**Walk away from the water on**
Water Street	**Centre Street to Water Street and**
1831-1835	**turn right. At the foot of William**
Private offices	**Street is the Double Bank**
HABS	**Building.**

This Greek Temple of early finance, originally home of the Merchants Bank on the south and Mechanics Bank on the north, now houses the Fishermen's Union and other fishing related interests. Appropriately located on Water Street, it is a reminder of the days when whaling was king, and Water Street was known as the Wall Street of New Bedford. It was the heart of banking and insurance interests as well as law offices and auction sites.

Architect Russell Warren designed the Greek Revival style structure, with its massive Ionic portico and polished granite steps and facade. It was built for the two original bank owners by two different builders. A disagreement between the builders arose, and the results can be seen by comparing the slightly different slope of the huge full height pillars. Reportedly only the four on the south are the correct interpretation of the architect's plan.

Rodman Candleworks

#15
Rodman Candleworks
Water and Rodman Streets
1810
Open as businesses
NRHP

Next on Water Street, across Rodman Street is the Rodman Candleworks.

The Rodman Candleworks, built in 1810, was one of the first in New Bedford to produce spermaceti candles, a major product of the whaling industry. Produced from raw sperm whale oil, these superior candles are dripless, smokeless, and burn twice as long as others of similar size. The intensity of light given off by the burning of one spermaceti candle was the original standard for one candle power.

Samuel Rodman, Sr. built the Candleworks after being associated with the Nantucket whaling oriented firm of his father-in-law, William Rotch, Sr. Rodman became a leading entrepreneur in New Bedford with his many whaling related ventures. He invested his large whaling profits in a new adventure called the textile industry, which ultimately became the mainstay of his family's fortunes. Samuel Rodman, Sr. incorporated his Quaker business ability, morality, and industry in all his public and private endeavors. Family and religion were basic in the business successes of these Quaker leaders.

When Samuel Rodman, Sr. died, his son-in-law Andrew

Robeson* picked up the reins at the Candleworks. Another son-in-law, Charles W. Morgan, had his office located here. Morgan was the owner of the famous whaling ship of the same name now on display at Mystic, Connecticut. Rodman's sons Benjamin (see New Bedford Glass Museum) and Samuel, Jr.* carried on the family traditions.

The Candleworks remained in the family until 1890. Subsequent uses included a mill workshop, warehouse, insurance offices, ships' bakery, contractor's office, antique store, and decorating studio. Finally damaged by fire and time, the building was abandoned in the 1960s.

The success story of the rehabilitation of the Rodman Candleworks demonstrates the power of coordinating public and private interests. City Community Development grants spurred rehabilitation efforts by ACT and WHALE*. ACT, Architectural Conservation Trust for Massachusetts, is the first state-wide, private, non-profit, revolving fund in the United States. ACT's president, Roger Webb, has been involved in the exterior rehabilitation of the Benjamin Rodman House*, authored the feasibility study for Boston's Quincy Markets, and developed Boston's old City Hall. The Rodman Candleworks renovation is a pilot project for ACT and will become a national model.

Adaptive reuse has drawn the New Bedford Five Cents Savings Bank to the Waterfront Historic District where they occupy the first and second floors of the Rodman Candleworks building and plan to open a walk-in bank appropriately styled in the mid-1800s. The bank, in returning to the financial center of the 1800s, demonstrates the re-establishment of historical ties between the Waterfront and Downtown, and strengthens both. The Candleworks' top floor will contain offices with a gourmet restaurant on the basement or ground floor.

The strong, Federal style structure has two-foot thick, native granite rubble walls with stucco facing, scored to resemble granite blocks. The windows and arched doors are detailed with rough cut granite quoins repeated at the building's corners. The top story has small lunette windows with surmounting keystones. The unusual color is the result of careful research and believed to be authentic.

Erected by New Bedford whaling and textile pioneers, scene of a variety of New Bedford business ventures, survivor of fire and time, innovatively and uniquely rehabilitated, the Rodman Candleworks takes its solid place in the revitalized Waterfront District.

NEW BEDFORD WATERFRONT

Access to the actual working waterfront and the open space boardwalk park is available via the Pedestrian Overpass. The Overpass, with its Observation Deck, can be reached from Rodman Street east of the Candleworks. For numbers 16 through 22 see Historic Districts Map, page 12.

Along the actual waterfront you become vitally aware of the throbbing heartbeat of New Bedford. From the mid 1700s, when Joseph Russell III, John Loudon, and Joseph Rotch first launched their fishing and whaling boats, up through today's multi-million dollar catch, the harvest of the sea has been the backbone of New Bedford's economy. The Acushnet River has long been the avenue from which fishing and whaling ships have plied the seven seas in search of the illusive yet priceless whale and ever present and essential seafood. Today New Bedford is the scallop capital of the United States and the leading port on the east coast in dollar value of catch.

The Acushnet River has also been the artery through which New Bedford has carried on a prosperous foreign trade and her ships have taken part in historic events. One of the early ships to sail from this port was the *Dartmouth,* built by the Rotch family in 1767 and later made famous as one of the ships of the Boston Tea Party. Here too in May 1775 the first naval encounter of the Revolution took place. Word was brought to a group of local militiamen that a sloop had been captured by Captain Linzee of the British ship, *Falcon.* New Bedford men quickly pressed the local sloop, *Success,* into service. Under cover of fog they surprised and captured a sloop which had been commandeered by the British, as well as found and re-captured their own sloop. This ended the first naval skirmish with victory for the colonists. Another Rotch ship, the *Bedford,* captained by Isaiah Burgess, was the first American ship to carry the new flag up the Thames River to London following the Revolution. Feelings were still running high when the *Bedford,* carrying oil for sale to their former mother country, arrived on February 6, 1783, a full seven months before the final treaty was signed formally ending the Revolution. New Bedford thus led the way in indicating that, though young, the United States was ready to take its place among the trading nations of the world.

To be part of this thriving, productive, and historic seaport, it is necessary to walk her waterfront. Here you are caught up in the work-a-day world of the fishermen, with its excitement and its drudgery, its dangers and its rewards. New Bedford's waterfront remains the active commercial fishing center it has been for more than 200 years.

#16

Fish Pier	Starting at the overpass from
On the Waterfront by the	Rodman Street take the Water-
Rodman Street overpass	front Boardwalk to the river's
Open all year, no fee	edge and the Fish Pier.

Once two separate piers, they are now combined into one large open pier with easy vehicular access to provide better service for New Bedford's fishing fleet and the daily auctions at Wharfinger's, the brick building adjacent to the pier. Of her approximately 150 vessels, roughly one third can be found in port at any given time. You will see them tied up two, three, and four abreast here and at the many wharves on both sides of the river. A fishing vessel is usually out for seven to ten days and in port for three.

Early in the morning the pier reaches its peak of activity when fishing and scallop boats, in with a fresh catch, tie up to await the auctions at Wharfinger's. Along the many piers can be seen boats of all types and conditions from $300,000 draggers to million dollar scallopers, from rusty hulls with peeling paint showing years of hard work and wear to new steel hulled ships sporting polished wood and shining mariner's enamel, and with names varying from *Pilgrim's Progress* to the *Atlantic Challenger, Theresa R.* and *Flying Dutchman.*

At night the pier is dramatically lit with lights high above the fishing boats, silhouetting them against the night sky. Wharfinger's is silent now after the day's hurried activity — quietly awaiting the seven o'clock scallop auction and the onset of another day in the vital life of New Bedford's fishing industry. In summer boats rock gently at their moorings, while in winter riggings are often coated with ice, reflecting the many difficulties of the year round harvest of the sea.

A meaningful monument to men who lost their lives at sea can be seen adjacent to the Overpass on the road side of the pier. Many go down to the sea in ships, but not all return, for feeding mankind is a hazardous business pursued only by men of courage and determination.

New Bedford fishing fleet

#17
Wharfinger Building
Scallop and Fish Auctions
Fish Pier
1934
Admission by permission of
  Fishermen's Union

Wharfinger's is found on Fish
Pier opposite the Coast Guard
Memorial.

At the base of Fish Pier sits Wharfinger's, an unassuming brick building with attractive dormers and a grey slate roof built in 1934 for the harbor master. Though one of the smallest structures on the waterfront, it is undoubtedly the most important. For here is decided the economic fate of every ship's load of scallops and fish. The price set for the world on scallops and yellow tail flounder is determined here in New Bedford each morning. The scallop auction is at 7:00 a.m. and the fish auction at 8:00 a.m. By their appointed time, the fishing captains, some still clad in boots and working clothes, crowd into the building to learn the fate of their catch. Each catch is listed on a board, a bell rings, and in less than a minute representatives from the processing plants have registered their bids. The captains then have fifteen minutes to decide if they will accept the bid price for their catch. Another bell rings, and the auction is finalized. Seven to ten days' work is decided in a few short hectic minutes. The boats then move to the processing plants at South Terminal where the catch is unloaded, processed, and shipped out by truck the same day. Another cycle in the life of the fishermen is completed.

Over fifty-four million dollars was the value of the catch in 1978. Through related industries this resulted in roughly 150 million dollars to the economy of New Bedford. Fresh seafood continues to be vital to the life of the city.

#18
Coast Guard Com-
  memorative Exhibition
Lightship *New Bedford*
Foot of Union Street, north
  side State Pier
1976
Open seasonally, fee charged

The Coast Guard Memorial is just
south of Wharfinger's on State
Pier.

Moored next to the working vessels she once protected is the now retired Lightship *New Bedford.* The bold red hull has tall

Lightship **New Bedford**

white letters marking the lightship which now draws visitors from all parts of the globe. When on duty, she drew the attention of world traveling mariners to the hazards of the sea. Her beacons, powerful enough to pierce the dense New England fog, and her foghorns, thunderous enough to penetrate the howling winds, are at rest now.

Visitors are encouraged to come aboard and explore the bridge, decks, chain lockers, quarters, windlass, galley, wardroom, and engine room. Here you can picture life aboard a lightship. A lightship was heavily anchored in dangerous waters as a lonely sentinel during all weathers and seasons. Her radio beacon, fog horn, and lights guided countless numbers to safety. Used as vital navigational aids, lightships were stationed in strategic places too difficult for a lighthouse. Now only two of the original fifty-six lightships remain in service, the rest having been replaced by automated monster buoys and light towers.

The Lightship *New Bedford* has served in the threatening waters of Nantucket Shoals, called the crossroads of the Atlantic. She has also seen duty off Portland, Maine, and served as a relief vessel where needed. Now a living memorial to Coast Guardsmen, she is appropriately stationed here. New Bedford, whose life has so long been oriented to the sea, was the first winter home of the Coast Guard Academy. In 1876 the idea was established to have a two year training of cadets from which to draw officers. The first school of instruction, an old schooner, was soon replaced by the new bark *Salmon P. Chase*. With the *Salmon P. Chase* in winter quarters in New Bedford, the school continued in a sail loft. The training school evolved into the now well known Coast Guard Academy in New London, for which this exhibition is a centennial commemorative.

The geodesic dome, part of the Coast Guard Commemorative on State Pier, could easily symbolize a Fresnel lens, which is used in lighthouses to concentrate and intensify the light beam. Under this symbolic dome are housed special exhibits of the Coast Guard including a thirty-six foot, self-righting rescue boat. Coast Guard cutters are stationed in this sea-oriented city, which is proud to retain her ties with the Coast Guard.

#19
State Pier   The State Pier is adjacent to the
                                    Coast Guard Memorial.

State Pier, operated by the Commonwealth of Massachusetts, with 1700 feet of berthing space, serves as the freight terminal for foreign and domestic goods passing through the port of New Bedford. Freighters from all over the world tie up here, with the largest number coming from South America.

The pier is also home to three US Coast Guard cutters, *Bibb, Unimak,* and *Vigilant,* which serve vessels in distress as well as help maintain control of the 200 miles offshore fishing areas from Canada to Florida. The Coast Guard's long and proud history is intermingled with that of New Bedford's. For it was here, aboard the training ship *Salmon P. Chase,* that the US Coast Guard Academy was born in 1876.

On the State Pier, in addition to large freighters unloading their international cargo, you can see fishing boats docking just long enough to sell their shack fish (extra seafood brought up with their main catch) to truck buyers. From this vantage point, enjoy the beautiful, protected harbor, with its varied fishing fleet hugging the docks on both sides of the river. The steepled skyline of Fairhaven is a backdrop on the far shore. Then look back at the panorama of New Bedford, with her conflicting yet seemingly

Fisherman icing down fishing boat prior to a trip

harmonious architecture, from the modern super highway ramps and office buildings to the domed top of the Whaling Museum and the restored nineteenth century buildings of the waterfront.

#20

Steamship and Coal Pocket Piers

South of State Pier are Steamship and Coal Pocket Piers.

Steamship Pier in earlier years served as a docking terminal for ferries running between New Bedford, Martha's Vineyard, and Nantucket. From 1891 until 1933 large white, side-wheelers proudly steamed between the islands and New Bedford, adding glamor and excitement to this, their home port. Following World War II a more modern type car and truck ferry was introduced. While improving efficiency, they never really filled the void of the picturesque side-wheelers, *Monnohansett* and *Martha's Vineyard,* and before long people found it just as easy to drive to Woods Hole for passage to the islands. By 1961 the Nantucket-New Bedford run was cancelled. Today ferries still leave during the summer months for Martha's Vineyard and Cuttyhunk, but from Leonard's Wharf.

The pier immediately south, Coal Pocket Pier, was a receiving point during the golden days of whaling for thousands of barrels of whale oil. Then later in the late 1800s the dock held high containers or pockets where coal was received and stored until being shipped out for local use by wagon — thus the name Coal Pocket Pier.

Until recently, Coal Pocket's lower styled wharves were ideal for local lobster boats. At present they are being converted to receive small commercial boats, including the lobster boats, as well as serving as a municipal type pier where pleasure, charter, and sight-seeing boats can tie up while visiting New Bedford. Possible future plans call for the berthing of historically significant ships which would be open for the education and enjoyment of the public. Steamship and Coal Pocket Piers will be a recreational window on a working waterfront.

#21
Bourne Counting House
Durant Sail Loft
Merrill's Wharf (also
    called Homer's Wharf)
1847-1848
Open as businesses
NRHP

The next wharf south is Merrill's or Homer's Wharf, on which the Bourne Counting House is located.

The massive granite block structure seemed indestructible, even when it was a neglected, fire-damaged, boarded-up derelict. Rescued and rehabilitated, the Bourne Counting House now features quality shops, an inn, and a top floor restaurant or lounge, with a magnificent panoramic view of the harbor and city.

The impressive building was constructed by Captain Edward Merrill on the wharf he had built between 1843 and 1847. Captain Merrill was a whaling vessel master before entering the oil and candle business in New Bedford. His 1837 late Federal home is located at 43 Seventh Street. At his wharf more whale oil was landed than anywhere else in New Bedford. The wharf eventually became the property of the city after Merrill's death.

In this sturdy, indomitable building were established the counting rooms of the legendary Jonathan Bourne in 1848, and here they remained until his death, over forty years later. Jonathan Bourne owned "more whaling tonnage than any other

Bourne Counting House   *(During restoration)*

man in this country, if not the world."⁹ This most successful whaling merchant began his career in New Bedford at age seventeen by clerking in a grocery business. He came from an industrious, self-reliant farming family in Bourne, a town which was later named for him.

Whaling was declining at the time of the Civil War, and many vessels were sacrificed in the stone fleet blockade of Charleston and Savanah Harbors. Bourne's optimism spurred the industry when he added five ships to his fleet at a time when others were cutting back. He further aided New Bedford's economy with his financial guidance of the textile industry which rapidly filled the gap left by whaling. Bourne was also an interested and powerful politician, a long time alderman, state representative, and member of the Governor's Council. His business interests included: railroads director, bank president and director, president of Bourne Mills in Fall River, and director of many other Fall River corporations. In New Bedford he was a director of mills, utilities, railroads, and a steamboat company.

The building remained an integral part of New Bedford's sea-oriented life when later used for sewing sails and known as the Durant Sail Loft in the first part of this century. In 1934 the sail loft made the sails for the *Charles W. Morgan* when she was an-

Charles W. Morgan, *last of the wooden whalers on the East Coast.*

chored at Round Hill in South Dartmouth before New Bedford lost her to Mystic, Connecticut. These sails, made for one of the last remaining wooden whale ships, were probably the only sails made for a whaler in half a century.

The one acre area known as Merrill's Wharf Historic District, and locally called Homer's Wharf, is listed in the National Register of Historic Places. Restoration plans involved retaining as much of the original building as possible. Included will be a replica of the second floor bay window purported to be used by Jonathan Bourne to note the arrival and departure of whaling vessels, many of which he owned. Community Development funds of the city provided exterior restoration. The adapted present use makes it again a vital part of this active Historic District.

#22

Leonard's Wharf **Adjacent to and south of Homer's Wharf and the Bourne Counting House is Leonard's Wharf.**

On Leonard's Wharf as much as anywhere else on the waterfront you can step into the world of the fisherman. Walk among

New Bedford fishing fleet

the fishing boats, observe how they work, and note the important mechanisms such as radar and sonar gear, trawling nets, scallop draggers, and dinghies perched in many cases safely atop cabin roofs. You quickly realize that, unlike pleasure boats, everything here has a purpose. There are few frills.

Over the years this present wharf has assumed the name of Leonard's Wharf, though it is not the original wharf of that name, which was situated further south on the river. The original Leonard's Wharf was named for Samuel Leonard, founder of the company which became Greene and Wood Lumber Company. It was the scene of a prosperous and extensive lumbering business, which came to the waterfront in 1840. Lumber from Maine, Florida, and the Gulf ports was brought here where it was processed through a large planing mill. By 1926 it was necessary to deepen the docking area and modernize their facilities to accommodate large steamers from the Pacific coast. The air was full of sawdust and the sound of screeching saws as loads of raw wood were transformed into carefully processed building materials. On either end of the dock could be seen huge derricks and cranes moving the wood from incoming ships, through the milling plant, and onto fleets of trucks for delivery. It was a very different scene from today's modern restaurant and commercial

79

fishing boats.

Leonard's Wharf, recently rehabilitated, illustrates an affable combination of work and pleasure. Along with the commercial fishing boats are docked ferries which offer daily trips, providing an enjoyable link with Martha's Vineyard and Cuttyhunk.

#23

Hurricane Barrier	**From Leonard's Wharf notice the**
Open access all year,	**protected harbor entrance. For**
building by appointment	**access to Barrier, see directions**
	with #65.

Never again will ships be broken against wharves, bulkheads twisted and toppled, buildings moved off their pilings, or riverside factories flooded here in New Bedford. For in 1966 this 9,100 foot long hurricane barrier, standing twenty feet above median sea level, was built through the combined efforts of local, state, and federal agencies. The disastrous effects of the 1938 and 1954 hurricanes and the fact that the city lies in a flood plain precipitated the building of this multi-million dollar barrier. The wall runs from Fort Phoenix in Fairhaven, across the river to Clark's Point, and along the inside of Clark's Cove to Rice Street. Flood gates are located at the river's entrance, on Rodney French Boulevard, and Cove Road.

The opening consists of two 400 ton gates, each operated by its own twenty-five horsepower motor. Under normal conditions a strobe beacon flashes three times per minute. This is increased to every three seconds when closing, and a constant flashing is shown while the gates are closed. There are also audible alarms and radio announcements. Only once has a ship ignored the signals and been caught in the gates . This was on January 23, 1966, when the *Nepco* leaving New Bedford, loaded with 6,500 barrels of oil, became wedged in the moving gates. Since that time the gates have successfully closed, protecting the inner harbor, as many as twenty-four times in one year.

The barrier is manned twenty-four hours a day and is in constant communication with the US Army Engineers Division at Wareham on the Cape Cod Canal. By order of the Corps of Engineers or by local decision, the hurricane gates can be closed in twelve minutes. When the direction and force of the wind, tide height, and weather conditions combine to threaten the inner harbor, the order is given, and the hurricane gates are closed.

Hurricane Barrier

Top of Hurricane Barrier

Thus New Bedford and its harbor, like a walled city of Jericho, are protected from the raging sea.

On calm days the top of the barrier, looking like the Appian Way in Rome, provides a perfect place for harbor viewing, walking, or fishing. Looking out to sea you can see Sconticut Neck on the Fairhaven side, and further out part of Cape Cod and the Elizabeth Islands, with Martha's Vineyard showing on the horizon.

The barrier itself is illuminated at night by a line of white lights. The opening is designated by a blinking green light on the returning port side and by red lights on the starboard side, welcoming home the ocean-weary sailors. Once inside the gate the seamen know they are safe from wind, tide, and storm, a truly sheltered port. It is one of the few on the New England coast that can offer such a guarantee.

#24
Palmer Island   Palmer Island is just inside the
Palmer Island Lighthouse   Hurricane Barrier.
1849

Picturesque Palmer Island, with its sentinel light, served as the gateway to New Bedford and Fairhaven's inner harbor before the Hurricane Barrier was built in 1966. From 1849 until 1966 the light shone like a familiar old friend, welcoming mariners on their run into the harbor.

The six-acre island, once covered with cedar trees, has had an interesting history. It was named for William Palmer, one of the original settlers living in Dartmouth in 1670, who was later scalped by Indians. Long before the island was home to Palmer Island Light, possibly as retribution for William Palmer, it served as a detention camp for captured Indians during King Philip's War in 1675-76. Indian fighter Captain Benjamin Church sent several groups of Indians here, among them the wife and son of Indian chief King Philip. The island was also ideally located for a garrison which offered protection to colonists during the continuing Indian Wars.

In 1849, encouraged by local seamen and also concerned with marine safety, the government erected a lighthouse on the extreme northeast tip of the island. William Sherman served as its first keeper.

It is hard to believe, looking at this deserted island, that over the years it has supported a lighthouse and keeper's family, a hotel, dance hall, bowling alley, and an amusement park. George Furber built a summer home here in 1866, which he converted to a hotel, and later added a dance hall. Ships transported customers between the island and New Bedford, and many a returning seaman enjoyed a visit to the island on his way into port. By 1890 the hotel business had fallen off, and Abbott P. Smith bought the hotel for a summer home. About the same time a bowling alley and amusement park were built on the southern end of the island. They lasted for several seasons, but the difficulty of getting people on and off the island led to their closing. In 1893 Dr. Ezekiel H. Noble tried once more to develop the island into a successful resort. Following his failure, the island was sold to Hathaway Manufacturing Company and Acushnet Mills Corporation to be used for coal storage. These plans were never carried out, and today it is owned by Norlantic Diesel Incorporated. The light itself is owned by the city which hopes to obtain ownership of the entire island in the near future.

The only remaining structure on the island is the lighthouse. Though charred and derelict, it speaks of a proud history. It was a guiding light for whalers during the years of New Bedford's greatest prosperity and has long welcomed mariners home after days and weeks at sea. Until 1941, when it was automated, a keeper and his family were always on duty. The last of the keepers was Arthur A. Small, who started his sea career at age fourteen sailing with the Maine and Gloucester fishing fleets. In 1906 he joined the navy and served in the Great White Fleet of Admiral Robley D. Evans. From there he moved to the Coast Guard and ultimately to the lighthouse service. In addition to being a talented seaman, he was also a gifted marine artist, who used his years of sea experiences as the background for his many canvasses.

Arthur Small and his wife Mabel served Palmer Island light from 1922 until the tragic hurricane of 1938. During the storm, Keeper Small lost his footing and was swept off the island. His wife, in a brave attempt to rescue him, tried to launch the dory only to be hit by a huge wave which washed her, along with the boathouse and keeper's house, into the raging river. Small, even after seeing his wife drown, somehow managed to retain consciousness and swim to the island. In spite of injuries and fatigue, he kept the light burning all night. The next day, rescued by friends, he requested to be relieved of duty before being taken to St. Luke's Hospital. Even in the face of injury and personal loss, he remained true to the traditions of the lighthouse service — that one never deserts a light until relieved, for its continued operation is essential to life and property.

Before you leave the waterfront area, let your mind slip back a century or more to the golden age of whaling, when ships' masts stood like a forest of trees against the skyline. Picture these wharves, busy with seamen from every port of call, with a mixture of strange accents and tongues intermingled with the Yankee twang. New Bedford was a town of seamen, wealth, and social prominence. It was a town of great contrasts, from the excitement and orderly confusion of the wharves with their smells of fish and whale oil, to the fragrant, manicured gardens and columned homes of the wealthy merchants, sea captains, and financiers. Then, as today, New Bedford was a town dependent on the sea.

#25

Andrew Robeson House
William and Second
  Streets
1821
Open as business in near
  future

Return via the Overpass from
Fish Pier to Rodman Street. Walk
up Rodman Street to Water
Street. Turn left and make an immediate right on William Street.
Continue up William two blocks
to the Andrew Robeson House on
the SE corner of William and Second Streets.

The unique, dominating, and beautifully proportioned Federal mansion draws your attention. It is truly symbolic of New Bedford, having been built by a prominent whaling and manufacturing entrepreneur and having been rescued and rehabilitated by the cooperative, mountain-moving efforts of the city and WHALE*.

Mountain-moving is an appropriate description, as this 700 ton ediface was painstakingly and at great risk moved here from its original site behind the Pairpoint Glassworks. Neither in-surance snags, doubting experts, Christmas shopping traffic, nor the wild winter of 1978 kept this mansion from its appointed new site. Twenty jacks and three winch trucks raised the unwieldy mass. Inch by inch, shredding nine green oak shoes on the way, it was moved 400 feet in four months. Winter was chosen as the best time, for the frost creates a "skin" which helps hold it together. The move was necessitated by the long-sought return to New Bedford of the Pairpoint Glassworks*. The return was contingent upon the glassworks' being able to use the space occupied by the Robeson House to construct necessary glass furnaces.

The mansion was first built in 1821 for Andrew Robeson. Robeson, successful in many financial areas, was described in the *Rich Men of Massachusetts* (1851) as "a great abolitionist, peaceman, Parkerite, and Democrat and yet, which is remarkable, very quiet and gentlemanly."[10] Originally from Pennsylvania, Quaker Robeson joined, through marriage, other prominent Quaker families, the Rodmans and the Rotches. Robeson had interests in whaleships, built a whale oil refinery, headed several banks, managed the Rodman Candleworks*, and founded a pioneering calico print works in Fall River.

His appropriately magnificent mansion was originally built near Second Street opposite the home of his brother-in-law, Ben-jamin Rodman*. The mansion was surrounded by stately gardens covering two city blocks. It was constructed with large, flat pieces of chlorite rock forming the rubblestone walls, which are faced with brick brought individually wrapped from Robeson's native Philadelphia. Simply ornamented with an unusual eliptical fanlight and brick arches surmounting the entrance and lower windows, the mansion has a Dutch cap (hip) roof and European glass remaining in some windows. All of the main rooms retain their fireplaces, marble mantels, and most of the woodwork.

By 1880 brick business buildings covered the once elegant gardens, and the mansion was hidden, used as a warehouse, and neglected. The area was known as the Robeson Block when it became the first commercial block in New Bedford. The mansion was later rescued and moved in 1978 to take its present place of honor in the Waterfront Historic District. The restored mansion, adapted for reuse as offices and apartments, stands as a magnificent example of the value of preservation.

#26
New Bedford Institution for Savings
Third District Court of Bristol
33 William Street
1853
Open as business, museum
NRHP, HABS, NHL

The New Bedford Institution for Savings is across the street on the NE corner of William and Second Streets.

The brown hued, cut stone facade and simple yet solid lines set the character of this structure which stands firm through its many uses. From the dignity of its origin as a pace setting bank and later a courthouse, through its use for shops and businesses, the building has evolved full cycle and is now being rescued and restored to its full status as a valued bank. The pioneering New Bedford Institution for Savings, which erected the building here in 1853, has recently repurchased its former home. Plans call for a limited teller bank operation with the rest a savings bank museum, the first in the country.

When the New Bedford Institution for Savings was created in 1825, its aim was to provide for the saver of moderate means at a time when commercial banks were for the wealthy. It was one of the few in the state with that purpose. Deposits were invested in local commerce, mainly related to whaling. The bank remain-

New Bedford Institution for Savings

ed here for nearly half a century. Next the building housed the Third District Court of Bristol from 1899 until 1914. In 1916 it was auctioned to the Nonquitt Tribe of Red Men and has served a variety of businesses since.

Built in 1853, designed by noted architect Russell Warren, the structure combines Greek and Italian Renaissance Revival styles. Ornamental heavy stonework flanks the central entry stairs, extending the granite foundation line. The shape of the pediment over the front entry is repeated in the larger pediment crowning the front facade. The dentil course in the upper pediment is similar to that of the Pantheon in Rome.

U.S. Custom House

#27

U.S. Custom House	The U. S. Custom House is on the
Second and William Streets	SW corner of William and
1834-1836	Second Streets.
Open all year, no fee	
NRHP, HABS	

Flying tall, high above the U. S. Custom House, are the stars and stripes and the colorful emblem of the United States Custom Office. The impressive Greek Revival style Custom House is appropriate for this successfully sea-oriented city. It was here that sea captains of old called to enter and clear their ships and cargo, and seamen from the world came to register for their papers. This largest and most elaborate of the four New England custom houses has retained its initial function for over a century. It is now the oldest custom house to continue in the United States.

At one time the United States Post Office was housed here. Now the concerns dealt with here are the logging and collecting of duties and tariffs, the Coast Guard vessel documentation, National Marine Fisheries Service, and foreign travel.

Congress designated the need for a custom house in 1789.

This New Bedford structure was designed by Washington Monument architect Robert Mills and possibly Russell Warren and was built between 1834 and 1836 at a total cost of $32,000. The front facade is carefully hewn, white granite and varied stone texture. The dominating classic style portico is supported by four massive Doric columns of tooled granite. The cupola provided a watch point with its harbor view. The interior features an unsurpassed cantilevered stairway; its solid stone worn by visitors from all over the world. The quoined vaulted ceilings are of special note.

#28

New Bedford Glass Museum	**Walk north on Second Street. On**
Benjamin Rodman House	**the right side is the New Bedford**
50 Second Street	**Glass Museum. The entrance is in**
1820-1821	**the rear, and parking is available.**
Open all year, fee charged	

Here in the New Bedford Glass Museum you can see and appreciate the beauty and superior craftsmanship of the Pairpoint, Mount Washington, and Gundersen Glass Works. In 1976 when the New Bedford Glass Society, with the help of community support, restored the Rodman House, a new star rose on the horizon of historic preservation. In this history laden house developed a museum of silver and fine glass work. The collection illustrates unique beauty in varying hues, designs, textures, cuts, and engravings. Pieces designed for queens, presidents, and other famous people are on display. Such famous glass majesty as Burmese, White Lusterluss, Alice-Blue, Peachblow, and Lava glass come alive to the museum visitor, as do the tools which were used in the making of such masterpieces.

Two historic preservation dreams, the founding of the New Bedford Glass Society and the restoration of the Rodman House, joined forces in the successful creation of this museum. In 1974 George Avila, now director, was instrumental in obtaining a charter for the New Bedford Glass Society. The founding members wanted to preserve and display the artistic history of glass making in New Bedford. They needed a building.

The Federal style Rodman House, the only waterfront mansion still standing on its own foundation, was built in 1820-1821 by Benjamin Rodman on land originally purchased by Joseph Rotch in 1765. Benjamin Rodman was an influential man in the town, being one of the founders of the New Bedford Institution

New Bedford Glass Museum (Benjamin Rodman House)

for Savings, vice president of the New Bedford Lyceum, and a member of the Committee of Vigilance, which was formed to protect the community from local class rioting. At one time he personally stood up to a mob that was about to burn a house in the waterfront area and demanded and received a lawful course of action.

This simple, dignified Quaker mansion, built of dressed granite blocks with quoined corners, was home to members of the Rodman family until 1872. Originally built with an impressive portico and graciously landscaped, by 1890 this once proud home was completely enclosed by store fronts. Its interior walls were removed for use as a warehouse. In 1965 Catherine Crapo Bullard freed the building from its foreign attachments and had the exterior restored. The hope was that it might be used as a museum for whaling mementos and city genealogical records. However, this idea did not materialize, and the house stood vacant until 1976 when the Glass Society, with the help of WHALE and Community Development Funds, purchased and restored the shell of the once beautiful home. It took nearly two years to reproduce the interior walls and woodwork and return the Rodman House to its past glory. On May 21, 1978, with historic chandeliers gleaming, treasured paintings on the walls, and display cases rich with glass, silver, copper, and brass, the museum within a museum opened. Two historic dreams had successfully united to preserve New Bedford's treasured and unique glass-making heritage along with one of her historic mansions.

#29
Pairpoint Glass works -   **Across the street is the Pairpoint**
     1894, 1977   **Glass Works.**
Bourne Warehouse - 1885
Second Street
Open - visitors welcome to
     observe craftsmen at
     work, no fee

The return of the Pairpoint Glass Works marked the renewal of glass artistry in New Bedford, for the history of Pairpoint Glass and the development of superior glass art are synonymous. Only by watching the artisans here at work can you truly appreciate the long hours and intricate steps that are involved in the making of a single piece of Pairpoint glass. Examples of the unusual hues and delicate designs as well as the historic progression of the company's creativity are on display at the Glass Museum across the street.

After a twenty-one year absence the company re-established itself in New Bedford when it leased the old Bourne Warehouse in 1977. With this move there came into play a unique advance in New Bedford's preservation history. The historically valuable Robeson House*, which was squeezed behind and attached to the Bourne Warehouse, was moved to the corner of William and Second Streets. This allowed room for Pairpoint to build a new glassworks and furnace room as well as to refurbish the 1885 Bourne Warehouse. The building has served over the years as a warehouse for auctioneer George A. Bourne, later home to the Safe Deposit National Bank, a motor repair shop, and now culminates its career as the new home of Pairpoint. This four story brick warehouse, which was built to last, will once again serve a thriving industry which is economically and historically important to New Bedford.

To understand the history of Pairpoint it is necessary to start with the New Bedford Glass Company, which was founded in 1866 by local businessmen and artisans. Three years later it was purchased by William L. Libbey, owner of the Mount Washington Glass Works in Boston and father of Edward Libbey, who

90

founded the famous Libbey Glass Works in Ohio. The Mount Washington Glass Company moved to New Bedford where the name soon represented outstanding craftsmanship and quality. Ten years later another company, Pairpoint Manufacturing Company, opened with Thomas J. Pairpoint as superintendent and head silver designer. As their silver earned world recognition, they became one of the largest manufacturers of silver plate in the country. In 1894 these two companies joined silver and glass artistry to form the Pairpoint Corporation. At the height of their prosperity they employed 2000 people and encompassed twenty buildings. Pairpoint then and now was synonymous with excellence.

The 1929 depression and the passing of the Reciprocal Trade Acts brought the once proud company to the doorstep of financial ruin. By 1939 it was bought by Issac N. Babbitt, Thomas A. Tripp, and Chester A. W. Best and named Gundersen Glass Works for Robert Gundersen, their top artist and gaffer. Upon Gundersen's death in 1952 the name Pairpoint returned to the company name as Pairpoint-Gundersen, which continued until 1956 when its door finally closed.

Later Robert Bryden bought the name and formulas and after several short term attempts opened a small factory in Sagamore, Massachusetts, on the Cape Cod Canal. Here success returned to the company, where glass was made for such well known names as Tiffany's and the Metropolitan Museum of Art in New York. It is this company, under the guidance of Mr. Bryden and the support of the Metropolitan Museum of Art, which has returned to New Bedford to continue a century of perfection in the glass industry. The famous Pairpoint trade mark " P " is once again placed on hand crafted glass artistry made in New Bedford.

#30
Haile Luther House
Second and Elm Streets
c1840
Open as business

Continue north on Second Street to the Haile Luther House on the SE corner of Second and Elm Streets.

The Haile Luther House, a fine Greek Revival, was saved from planned demolition and moved into the historic area by the combined efforts of the state, city, and WHALE*. Neatly rehabilitated, it serves as a quality shop with an apartment above.

The fine lines are highlighted by the grey trim against white clapboards. The side facing the Glass Museum features a Hathaway arch, where the edge of the window extends into the dormer. This arch seems to be found only in New Bedford. Built by its first owner, stonemason Haile Luther, the house has a roof with the true pitch of a Greek temple.

Haile Luther, a Quaker, was born in 1800 in Warren, Rhode Island. He was the son of shoemaker Barnabas Luther, who was a fifth generation descendant of original settler captain John Luther. In mid century he is believed to have joined the California gold rush, and by 1867 he returned to New Bedford to live with his son.

CENTRAL NEW BEDFORD HISTORIC DISTRICT

This district is frozen in time — representing the turn of this century, when New Bedford was first in the nation in fine cotton goods and yarn. This industrial prominence was reflected in the fine homogeneous downtown area this affluence produced. For, when whaling declined and the mills rose in importance, the center of business activity gradually left the waterfront and moved here.

Most building occurred between 1890 and 1910, with the already constructed library and City Hall being extensively and finally modified during that time. The library, once Greek Revival, was completely remodeled to the gravity and monumentalism of Egyptian Revival. Nearby, at 25 Sixth Street, the neoclassical Registry of Deeds building was built in 1908. The Masonic Building at Union and Pleasant Streets is interesting for the rare Italianate cast iron on the cornices and pilasters of the facade. Later, in 1913, the post office's classical Revivalism is a product of more modern technology, with all classical elements made by machine.

Banks are important in this district, such as the imposing New Bedford Institution for Savings built in the 1890s on Union Street across from the downtown shopping mall. The beginning of the Star Store, across from the bank, occurred at about the same time. Expanded in 1924 to its present size, it was then the largest department store in the country. In 1948 it installed the country's first escalator, which is still in operation today.

When New Bedford's economy suffered, these buildings were maintained rather than replaced. Today they provide the interesting picture of a small city's business and governing center at the turn of the center.

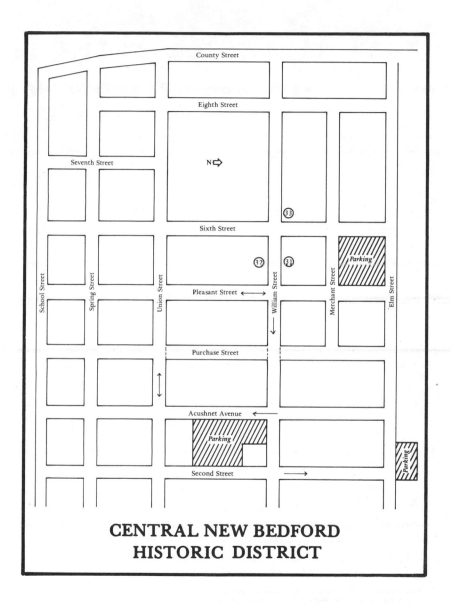

CENTRAL NEW BEDFORD
HISTORIC DISTRICT

City Hall

#31
City Hall
Pleasant, William, Sixth
　Streets
1856
Open

From the Haile Luther House return on Second Street to William Street, turn right, and walk up William Street. The City Hall is on the NW corner of William and Pleasant Streets

Note the detailed frieze in the pediment above the front entrance illustrating the important industries of New Bedford: fishing, whaling, textiles, shipping, and railroads. The motto on the New Bedford seal, "Lucem Diffundo" or "We light the world," is a living reminder of New Bedford's greatness as a whaling center, whose whale oil provided light for the world.

The cornerstone for today's neo-classical City Hall, designed by Solomon K. Eaton of Mattapoisett, was laid in 1856. City offices were housed on the first floor with the library on the second. Thanks to the many generous gifts to the library, prominent among these given by the Howland family, it became necessary to build a new wing in 1886 to house the additional books and supply adequate reading areas. The building was again enlarged in 1906 by local architect Samuel C. Hunt to its present structure. He raised the roof, made the external appearance of the second floor different from that of the first, moved the entrance to the west, and enhanced the brick facade by adding brownstone quoins to the corners. Hunt died in 1908 before the changes were completed. Egbert G. Bullard oversaw the finishing details and changed the Pleasant Street entrance, adding an egg and dart motif. Notice the unusual design of the elevator with its openness and convenient seating arrangement. Installed in 1906, it is the oldest functioning elevator in the United States — a tribute to its builder and to the care given it by an historically-oriented city.

Though additions and changes were made over the years by different builders and architects, the basic style and feeling of this stately City Hall have been retained, giving a feeling of permanence, solidarity, and strength.

#32
New Bedford Free Public
   Library
Pleasant and William
   Streets
1837
Open all year, Monday
   through Saturday, no fee

Across from the City Hall is the New Bedford Free Public Library.

The first library in New Bedford was created in the late 1700s when a group of young men pooled their books and opened a lending library. It was housed in a small building known as Federal Hall, near the corner of Union and County streets, which at that time was on the estate of William L. Rotch.

As literary interest grew in this economically and intellectually active town, several social libraries were organized, uniting in 1810 to form the New Bedford Social Library. It served the community well until 1851 when the Massachusetts General Court passed a law allowing the formation of free public libraries to be paid for by local governments. Accordingly, in 1852 New Bedford appropriated $1,500 for the formation of the Free Public Library in New Bedford, the first such public library to open in the commonwealth.

The library was housed from 1856 to 1910 on the second floor of the building that is now the City Hall. In 1910 the library was moved across the street to its present permanent home. The books were ingeniously propelled across William Street into a window of the present library by way of a chute.

This present library building was built in 1837 with funds given the town by the Federal government from surplus tax money. It was designed by architect Russell Warren and built of native granite with the two pillars brought from a Fall River quarry

95

New Bedford Free Public Library

Whalers' Memorial

by twenty teams of oxen. It served for years as the Town Hall and market place, with the market on the ground floor. Following a devastating fire in 1905, architect Nathaniel C. Smith added two wings and introduced Egyptian Revival architecture to the interior of this Greek Revival building. The small elevator in the library is the only known Egyptian Revival elevator in the world. In 1910 this building, demonstrating early adaptive reuse, became the library.

Today the library houses over 368,000 books, has an extensive genealogy department, and a special Melville Whaling Room containing one of the finest collections of written material on the whaling industry.

On the front lawn are two significant memorials. One is a bell given by Henry H. Hooper Company in memory of all who gave their lives in battle for this country. The second, given by William Wallace Crapo, represents the golden years of New Bedford as well as the undaunted spirit and courage of the whalemen, with the inscription "A dead whale or a stove boat."

#33
First Baptist Church
140 William Street
1829
Open for services all year
NRHP

Continue up William Street to the First Baptist Church on the right.

This white steepled, Federal and Greek Revival church stands as a monument to religious freedom, for the early settlers in the Dartmouth-New Bedford area were Baptists and Quakers seeking freedom from the Puritan-minded Plymouth settlement. The church can trace its history back to a Baptist minister, the Reverend John Cooke, who came to the new world as a boy aboard the *Mayflower*. He was one of the signers of the original deed for the Dartmouth territory purchased from the Indians in 1652 and an early representative to the General Court in Plymouth. The Reverend Cooke was active in founding, in 1685, the Baptist Church in Tiverton, at that time part of Dartmouth.

More than a century passed before eighteen members from the Tiverton Church met in New Bedford to organize their own church. Final action was taken at the home of James Tripp, and the First Baptist Church of New Bedford came into being June 30, 1813. The group, led by the Reverend George Hough, first met in Kempton Hall on Second Street. After eight months the Reverend Hough left to become a missionary to Burma, where he was the first to print the Bible in Burmese. Through his early

97

First Baptist Church

missionary actions, the Baptist Foreign Missionary Society was founded.

From Kempton Hall the congregation moved to the old Town Hall on Second and School Streets, where the congregation grew to a membership of 221 by 1828, at which time they incorporated. A year later they broke ground for the present building on William Street. The imposing, sky-reaching steeple of today's church has long served as a guide to mariners entering the Acushnet River. For this reason the steeple is prominently displayed as the central figure on the seal of New Bedford.

As the steeple has reached out to mariners, so the church has reached out to the community and established Baptist mission churches for Portugese, French, and Swedish speaking members during the 1890s. In the meantime they had established the North Baptist Church in 1872.

This classical church — with ship-lap front facade, Greek-styled columns, clapboard siding, hand blown glass windows, and cupola topped bell tower — has grown and changed over the years. It was enlarged in 1833, and the pulpit was moved from the south to the north end of the sanctuary in 1841. The vestibule and iron fence were built in 1856, and the Sunday School building, housing a memorial chapel, was dedicated in 1928. The steeple was destroyed by the 1938 hurricane and rebuilt in 1958. The interior was refurbished in 1966, only to be damaged by fire and restored to its present beauty in 1976-1977. Due to its historic and architectural interest, the church was placed on the National Register of Historic Places in 1975.

A noteworthy active member of the First Baptist Church, from 1862 to 1865, was Captain Henry Martyn Robert who served as a trustee. One evening, while conducting a church meeting on the defense needs of the harbor, he had trouble maintaining order. He had so much trouble that he was later inspired, in 1876, to write what became a basic text on parliamentary procedure, now known as *Robert's Rules of Order*.

These freedom-loving Baptists took an early stand against slavery with the Reverend John Girdwood preaching against the ills of slavery. As early as 1814 a Black, Mr. Isaac Thomas, was baptized and welcomed into the church membership, illustrating one more positive step in this city which respects all ethnic and religious backgrounds. Like their founding fathers, the members of the First Baptist Church believe in freedom of expression for all.

COUNTY STREET HISTORIC DISTRICT

County Street has long been an important artery in New Bedford's history. First it was an Indian trail, then it became the earliest road between Russell's Mills and Plymouth. In 1676, during King Philip's War, Captain Benjamin Church and Plymouth soldiers marched Indian prisoners along it on their way to Plymouth, where the Indians were tried and later sold into slavery in the West Indies. A century later it was used by the British during their 1778 invasion of New Bedford. Then in the 1800s County Street, running along the crest of the hill with its view of

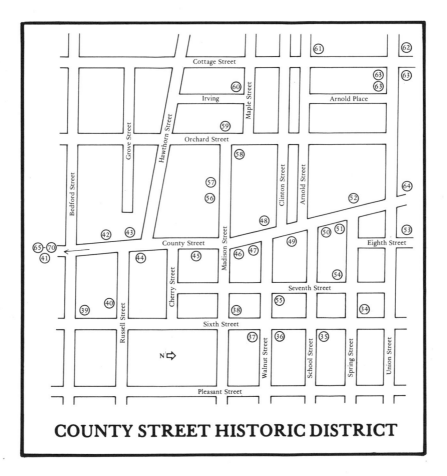

Cottage Street

Irving

Maple Street

Arnold Place

Grove Street

Hawthorn Street

Orchard Street

Bedford Street

Clinton Street

Arnold Street

County Street

Madison Street

Eighth Street

Cherry Street

Russell Street

Seventh Street

Sixth Street

Walnut Street

School Street

Spring Street

Union Street

N

Pleasant Street

COUNTY STREET HISTORIC DISTRICT

the harbor, became the chosen site of many grand residences of prosperous sea captains and merchants.

Between the Revolution and the War of 1812 profits from the sea were invested in homes nearer the waterfront. After the War of 1812 more prosperous homes were built on Sixth and Seventh Streets and finally on County Street itself. As greater wealth from the sea flowed into New Bedford, more substantial homes were built moving by neighborhoods from the first homes by the waterfront up the hill to the gracious mansions on County Street.

Many of the Federal period homes have been modified beyond recognition, especially in the areas nearest County Street. Greek and early Gothic Revival began appearing on County Street and west by the mid 1800s. Development of other elaborate Victorian styles continued west and filled in space within the County Street District. Little of the twentieth century has invaded this area, which now provides a route of fascinating exploration into the opulent architecture and grand achievements of New Bedford's whaling and mercantile captains and kings.

#34
Friends Meeting House
Spring Street
1785, c1822
Open for services

From parking area exit onto William Street going east toward the river. At bottom of hill turn right on Water Street and go to Union Street. Turn right on Union and continue west to Sixth Street. Turn left on Sixth. Park on Sixth near the corner of Spring Street. The Friends Meeting House is on the NW side of Spring Street.

Known as "Children of the Light" and "Friends in Truth", early Quakers first came to the Dartmouth area in 1664 seeking freedom from persecution by the Plymouth Colony. While in later years the town would grow and be strengthened by a variety of faiths, it was the early Quakers who first caused New Bedford to prosper. They were guided by their devotion to truth, strict discipline, unadorned way of life, belief that God revealed His plan as an inner light to individuals, eternal optimism, and belief

101

Friends Meeting House

in their own abilities. In the mid 1700s other Quakers came from Nantucket bringing with them an expertise in whale fishery. This knowledge — combined with the ethical, spiritual, and economic strengths of the Quakers — formed the solid foundation for New Bedford's greatness as the whaling capital of the world.

The Quakers built their first meetinghouse in the Apponagansett area of Dartmouth in 1699. By 1785 there were enough Quakers living in New Bedford to warrant the building of their own meetinghouse on Spring Street on land given by Joseph Russell III. By 1821 the Society of Friends had grown to 700 strong and a new building was needed. To make room for the proposed meetinghouse, the old one was moved to 17 Seventh Street, where it is now an apartment house.

This proved to be a time of mixed blessings for the Quakers. In 1822 when the new meetinghouse was built, they were at an all-time high in membership and in economic, political, and social prominence in New Bedford. Yet a schism was growing in the Society that within a year would cause an irreversible split in the group. While their original simplicity and oneness of purpose, in which they believed in absolute obedience to God's will with no exception, had been basic to their early strength, it was now beginning to cause disharmony. There were a growing number of more liberal-minded Quakers known as "New Lights" seeking greater freedom of emotional expression in their social life, speech, and way of dress. The strict orthodox Quaker, with his Biblical speech patterns, sombre clothing, and quiet gatherings, could not accept these inevitable changes. Thus the "New Lights", led by such prominent members as Mary and Elizabeth Rotch and Elizabeth and Benjamin Rodman, along with the Russell daughters, the Charles Morgans and James Arnolds, left the Society and joined with the Unitarian Church. From this time on, though Quakers continued to have a positive influence on the city, their strength of membership began to decrease. It is interesting to note that the exemplary lives of many a Quaker brought people to Christianity, but not necessarily as Quakers.

This present austere, brick building still welcomes Quakers today as it first did in 1822. Notice the two sets of hand chiseled stone steps leading to separate entrances — one for men and one for women. The simple severity of the structure is broken only by the slight curve in the stair railings. The inside is equally Spartan with simple glass fixtures, unadorned walls, plain molding around curtainless windows, and hand planed cushioned benches. In earlier days there was a partition that was lowered to separate the men and women during monthly business meetings. A unique feature of this meetinghouse is the sounding board for the benefit of deaf members.

The Quakers showed an early concern for the welfare of their fellowman. They were the main support of many local philanthropies and were deeply concerned with and became strongly opposed to slavery. Joseph Russell, John Howland, and Rebecca Slocum were the last to give up the use of slaves, but by 1785 all had — a full seventy-eight years before the Emancipation Proclamation. One of the early branches of the Anti-Slavery Society was established by the Society of Friends in 1834. Prior to the Civil War, Quakers were active in helping literally hundreds of slaves and in supporting the Underground Railroad.

The Friends Society believes that God's spirit is present in every person, and therefore they should be concerned with the welfare of all people. With the Quakers in New Bedford this was not just an idea, but a way of life.

Standish House

#35
Standish House
20 Sixth Street
c1825
Open as New Bedford
   Women's Club

Continue one block south on Sixth Street. The Standish House is on the left, NE corner of Sixth and School Streets.

A seventh generation descendant of Miles Standish, Levi Standish built this house about 1825. Levi was a successful grocery merchant during the peak days of whaling. The house remained in the Standish family until 1916, when purchased by the New Bedford Women's Club.

This fine Federal house of stately brick retains the fanlight above the entry, the small portico supported by two Ionic columns and pilasters, and a Dutch or low pitched hip roof. Of particular note is the delicately detailed wrought iron fence which is original.

#36
Francis Rotch House
223 Walnut Street
1803
Private

Continue one block south to Walnut Street. The Francis Rotch House is on the left, NE corner of Sixth and Walnut Streets.

Francis Rotch, who often strayed from his rigid Quaker background to follow the beat of a different drummer, was born on Nantucket in 1750 and came to New Bedford as a teenager with his father, Joseph, and brother, Joseph, Jr., in 1765. Though his father was the dominant force behind early New Bedford whaling, Francis also played an integral part in the family whale fishery enterprises.

In 1772 Joseph, Jr. died in England leaving Francis the majority of his estate, which included a brick warehouse and property in Boston. For this reason he was in Boston, overseeing his new property, when the famed tea ships, *Beaver, Dartmouth* (both Rotch ships) and *Eleanor* arrived from England in November, 1773. It was laid to Francis to save the ships and cargo if possible. He was caught between the British, who would not allow the ships to leave port without discharging all of their cargo, and the patriots led by Sam Adams, who strongly opposed the unloading of the symbolically tyrannical tea. Unable to obtain the necessary papers to clear the port, Francis was relieved of responsibility when the tea was adroitly cast into the sea water by patriots under the guise of Indians. As Francis' efforts had been above reproach by the patriots, his ships and other cargo were not harmed — a tribute to Francis.

Following the war he became involved in what proved to be an unsuccessful whaling operation from the Falkland Islands in the South Atlantic. From there he went to England and then to France, where for many years he had an interesting alliance with one Mme. Wilker Stork Haley Jaffrey. Here he helped manage the Rotch whaling fleets sailing out of Dunkirk, Nantes, and Le-Havre for more than twenty years. In 1809-1810 he returned to New Bedford and lived for a time with his older brother, William, Sr. In 1815 he married his cousin Nancy Rotch and three years later bought this home, then owned by Andrew Robeson. They lived here until his death in 1822.

Francis, the dreamer and inventor, was often frustrated as he tried to change or improve the technology of whaling. He applied for many patents both in France and in New Bedford. Sev-

Francis Rotch House

eral were in an effort to invent a self-propelled, two-hull boat called the *Roderick Dhue*, as well as other gadgets such as a whaling gun and boat pump operated by the boat's own motion. While it is true not all of his ideas were practical, any type of change met with strong resistance in that tradition-laden world of New Bedford. Undaunted even in his seventies, after signing his will aboard ship, he sailed off on the *Elizabeth* to try out one more method of whaling. Returning unsuccessful in his attempt to change traditional ways, he died two years later in 1822.

This Federal style house, which was built in 1803 by Nantucket whalesman Captain Andrew Swain, has been altered over the years. However, the windows, trim, cornerboards, and cornice are original. Francis' widow, Nancy, lived on here until her death in 1867. In later years it was residence to Mary Russell, one of the last descendants of the original Russell family, who died in 1928.

#37
David Coffin House
34 Sixth Street
1833
Private

David Coffin House is across Walnut Street on the left, the SE corner of Sixth and Walnut Streets.

There is a definite similarity between this brick Federal built here in 1833 and three identical Georgian style, brick mansions

David Coffin House

built on Nantucket Island in 1838 by David Coffin's distant cousin, Joseph Starbuck, for his three sons. The similarity continues as both families came from the island of Nantucket, were prosperous whaling merchants, and had the income to live in the gracious manner of the day.

The original Coffin house was surrounded by a comfortable amount of land, which has since been sold for building lots. The home, with its bridge chimneys set on parapet gabled ends, originally had shuttered windows and a balustrade at the roof level connecting the parapets. Notice the Greek Revival treatment of the front entrance and the large, windowed cupola, which must have given David Coffin an unobstructed view of the harbor and a chance to observe the safe return of his six whaling ships.

#38
George Howland, Jr. House
37 Sixth Street
1834
Private apartments

The George Howland, Jr. House is one block south on the right, the NW corner of Madison and Sixth Streets.

George Howland, Jr. developed the strong heritage of his family's economic prowess and prominence to become the leading force in New Bedford in the mid 1800s. He began with the Quaker education fitting for the son of a leading Quaker

107

George Howland, Jr. House

businessman. (See George Howland, Sr. House #54) and at fourteen joined his father's business. He continued in whaling and related concerns for over sixty years.

This handsome, likeable, intelligent, good humored man
successfully combined business and politics in a positive way. In
addition to his active whaling interests, he held long standing
positions in several banks and railroads. In New Bedford he was a
selectman and later mayor for five terms. He was a state representative, senator, and member of the Governor's Council. He
was on the executive committee on Indian Affairs for President
Grant. Here he spent time with the Osage Indians in Kansas com-
piling a fund of information. He was active in other government,
religious, charitable, and educational groups. He gave his salary
as mayor for two years to the New Bedford Library.

George, Jr. and his half brother Matthew continued whaling
investments after the 1840s prime. As late as 1867 they had the
beautiful whaler the *Concordia* built. It was a gallant gesture of
faith, a sense of Noblesse Oblige, a Howland tribute to their
nearly full century of successful whaling.

The house was originally set amid lovely gardens of half a
city block. A stately Federal with carriage houses, the estate was
appropriate for this leading New Bedford citizen. The roof balustrade, shutters, and extensive grounds are gone, and details such
as the Greek Revival front portico have been added. The true
lines of brick on its solid granite foundation remain. A wrought

iron fence and granite pillars define the property front. Now this modified late Federal is a fine example of New Bedford's surviving nineteenth century architecture.

One block over, at 46 Seventh Street, can be seen the interesting carriage house that originally belonged to this estate. Built at the same time as the main house, the style is a different variety of architectural combinations resulting in the Gothic Cottage effect. It is used today as a private apartment.

#39

New Bedford Fire Museum	Continue south on Sixth Street to
Bedford and Sixth Streets	Bedford Street. The Fire Museum
1866, 1880s, 1890s	is on the right, the NW corner.
Open seasonally and by	
appointment, fee charged	
NRHP	

The museum shares the building of Fire Station #4, the Cornelius Howland Engine Company. The company established in 1867 was the oldest active station in Massachusetts and possibly in New England until decommissioned in 1979. The Fire Museum tells the history and lore of early fire fighters and displays their meticulously maintained equipment, in interesting complement and contrast to the shiny modern, active engines of today. The bicentennial project museum spans the years of fire protection, service, and bravery, showing the development of city fire fighting techniques.

The visitor is guided by wall murals in three languages made at the Swain School of Design. Proudly gleaming ancient engines demand your attention. The huge 1855 New Bedford hand pump stands next to the 1866 steam pump which replaced it. The more modern 1884 engine was also housed here when in active service, and the 1934 engine served in the north end of the city. The shiny 1928 engine runs as smoothly as it did when on duty here until 1954.

Other displays tell the history of fire fighting and the pride, dedication, and courage of the fire fighters. Ancient fire buckets, tools, and models are here as well as trumpets which were used for communication during the battle against fire. Now symbolic, elaborate trumpets became fitting achievement and bravery awards and are displayed here along with other ornate and impressive awards, one from the old Pairpoint glassworks. Original

New Bedford Fire Museum

log books provide a fascinating study. Clothing is a main attraction with many varied pieces here, some available for interested children to try on. Other working exhibits to be tried are the pole to slide and bells to ring. Photographs augment the collection.

Cornelius Howland, Sr., a Quaker, was a vessel master who was captured during the Revolution and imprisoned in Edinburgh Castle for over a year. Ill, and given up for dead, he claimed he was miraculously revived by eating cherries. When a doctor munching cherries passed his death bed, Howland held out his hand into which the doctor placed his cherries, and his recovery soon followed. He had secreted a small amount of gold by passing it from one hand to another during searching. This he used to bribe a washerwoman, and he escaped in her clothes.

Fire Station #4 with its current emergency equipment occupies the oldest part of the building constructed in 1866. It is a two story brick structure with heavy granite lintels and hip roof. The museum side was once the old repair section and was added in the 1880s and 1890s with the front facade matching the Fire Station #4 side. It now serves as the interesting fire fighting museum and appropriate tribute to fire fighters everywhere.

#40

William Tallman Russell
   House
66-68 Russell Street
1822-1823
Private

While you are parked to see the Fire Museum walk back up Sixth Street one block to Russell Street and turn left. The William Tallman Russell House is the first house on the left facing Russell Street at number 66-68.

     William Tallman Russell was a shrewd merchant and shipowner, carrying on the successful traditions of the pioneering families from which he descended. Son of Gilbert and Lydia Tallman Russell, and grandson of Joseph Russell III, he married Silvia Grinnell of another strong New Bedford family. Educated in Friends' schools, he began his career as a counting room apprentice, later traveled, then commanded ships before branching out to other whale related interests.

     The house was built between 1822 and 1823 by Gilbert Russell for his son and daughter-in-law. Originally a Federal mansion surrounded by well maintained gardens of flowers and fruit trees, through the years the building was modified to a Greek Revival style, added to, and finally badly damaged by fire in 1977.

     WHALE* acquired the house after the fire and, by removing some later additions which suffered the most from the fire, restored it to the Greek Revival or Transitional stage. The gable facing the street is a massive forty-five feet long and is highlighted by the central eliptical fanlight. The full width porch is supported by four sets of double columns.

#41

St. John the Baptist Church
County and Wing Streets
1871, 1913
Open for services and
   meditation

Return to your car and continue south on Sixth Street to County Street and turn right. Drive one block north and the church is on the NE corner of County and Wing Streets.

     St. John the Baptist Church has the honor of being the first Portuguese Catholic church in the United States. Today's beautiful granite Romanesque church was completed in 1913, thus continuing services to a parish that began in 1871. The early

St. John the Baptist Church

members of this Portuguese parish attended St. Mary's Catholic Church in New Bedford during the mid 1800s. As more and more Portuguese came to the city they sought their own church, which became a reality on September 10, 1871. (For additional background information see pages 32-33.)

To fully appreciate this Mother church of the Portuguese churches in the city, it is necessary to step inside. The altar area is highlighted with beautiful murals depicting special events in the life of Christ, the Stations of the Cross are meaningfully done in relief, and the bold brilliant colors of the stained glass windows all add to your appreciation of the beauty, solemnity, and spiritual strength that is here. St. John the Baptist Church, like the other twenty-some Catholic churches in the city, provides a spiritual center for its parishioners. These many Catholic churches have all had a strong positive influence on the city of New Bedford since the mid 1800s.

#42
Joseph Grinnell Mansion
379 County Street
1832
(for sale, future use
   unknown)
HABS

Return to your car and turn right on Bedford Street and go to County Street; turn right. The Joseph Grinnel Mansion will be on the left next to Joseph Kennedy Youth Center.

Joseph Grinnell, successful manufacturer, astute businessman, and able politician, came from an old Massachusetts family. Joseph's father was Cornelius Grinnell, a Revolutionary Period privateer, noted sea captain, and successful businessman. His brother, Cornelius, Jr., built his mansion nearby at the corner of County and Hawthorn Streets. "Grinnell Land", a memorial in the Arctic, is dedicated to the Grinnell family as an ancestor, Henry Grinnell, actively encouraged Arctic expeditions.

Joseph Grinnell, whose life spanned nearly a century, was launched on his career as a clerk for his father and uncle. Later he formed a company in New York with an Howland uncle. The Howland and Grinnell company owned vessels, most of which were captured or confiscated during the war of 1812. In New Bedford he formed other businesses, one with a cousin named Captain Preserved Fish. He was president of the First National Bank and of the New Bedford and Taunton Railroad. He was in-

Joseph Grinnell Mansion

strumental in founding the Wamsutta Mills and became its first president. He was a member of the Massachusetts Governor's Council and served four terms in the United States House of Representatives. His valuable knowledge of mercantile affairs was a great boon to New Bedford's development.

Grinnell's austere yet imposing mansion of Quaker precision and simplicity was designed by Russell Warren. That noted architect contributed many fine buildings to New Bedford, primarily as a result of Joseph Grinnell's patronage. Originally Greek Revival in style, the solid, massive, granite ashlar square is dominated by the giant Doric portico. The full height, supporting fluted Doric columns, were destroyed by fire, and the square shaft replacements are not replicas of the originals. The wooden third floor was added in 1893 when the gable was removed. The rough-cut granite, hauled by oxen, came from the

Quincy quarry which supplied the granite for Boston's Bunker Hill monument. Some of the earlier elegance remains in the tall rounded mahogany doors with silver door knobs and in the intricate oak leaf moldings.

Christmas Day in 1832 was the scene of the Joseph Grinnells' occupation of their new home. Here they hosted John Q. Adams, Daniel Webster, and Abraham Lincoln, among others. The mansion remained in the family until 1940, when it was given to St. John the Baptist Church. The stately mansion became a school and later a youth center. During World War I the Red Cross used a part of the building for workrooms and storage. In 1931 it was badly damaged by fire and later modified for its use as a school. It remains a fine example of New Bedford's interest in classical architecture and the ability of her citizens to afford it.

#43

Cornelius Grinnell, Jr.
   Mansion
Ahavath Achim Synagogue
County and Hawthorn
   Streets
1828
Open for Synagogue services

The Cornelius Grinnell, Jr. Mansion is part of the Ahavath Achim Synagogue and is the next house on the left at the SW corner of County and Hawthorn Streets.

Little is known of Cornelius Grinnell, Jr. who purportedly committed suicide soon after this mansion was built. Brother of Joseph,* he was the son of Cornelius Grinnell, an early Revolutionary privateer who was considered a most reliable ship captain of the old school. The senior Cornelius Grinnell was captured and held prisoner during his privateering days. He and others had an elaborate escape plan involving capturing a schooner, kidnapping the governor of the island on which they were detained, and bringing both to Boston or New York. The plan nearly succeeded. It was sabotaged by the conscience of one of the conspirators, who revealed it to the governor who had been nice to them. After his eventual release, Cornelius Grinnell sailed as first mate and later as captain of the *Rebecca,* which claims the first Pacific whaling voyage. He was also a pioneering bank director and involved in the incorporation of another bank. Using his mind and energy well, Cornelius Grinnell made his own niche. He was forceful and hearty, yet polished, neat, and always in good taste.

Later in the mansion's history it was owned by Miss Ellen R. Hathaway, sold by her heirs, and in 1939 became the property of the congregation of this synagogue. The mansion itself contains the main assembly room with a balcony created by removing part of the second floor. Brought from their old building, a Pairpoint crystal chandelier hangs above the tabernacle. In 1962-1963 the attached Hebrew school and chapel were constructed.

The history of Jews in New Bedford dates back to 1748, when the earliest Jews were of Spanish and Portugese descent and came here from Newport. Aaron Lopez, a Spanish Jew and refugee from the Spanish Inquisition, became a partner of Francis Rotch, fitted out about forty whaling ships, and made a fortune in sperm oil candles. The Revolutionary period's destruction of the whaling fleet wiped him out. By the 1860s economic conditions forced Jews away. Traditionally, the last to leave gave the cemetery key to Mayor Rodney French with instructions to give it to the first Jew to resettle. Finally, about 1890, a small number of Jews banded together to form the first congregation which has seen much strong growth since. They met in several places before finding their home in the Cornelius Grinnell, Jr. Mansion.

The land on which the mansion stands was given the first owner by his father-in-law, Gilbert Russell.* The simple, plain, white clapboard structure is ornamented only by the interesting portico with supporting columns and pilasters. It is fronted by the original wrought iron fence and stone walls. Its simplicity is in marked contrast with the Joseph Grinnell* mansion of Cornelius Junior's brother at nearby 379 County Street.

#44

William R. Rodman Mansion
Swain School of Design
388 County Street
1833
Open during school hours

The William R. Rodman Mansion is on the right side of County Street at the head of Hawthorn Street.

When you look at this imposing Greek Revival mansion — with its six impressive fluted columns topped by Corinthian capitals and its setting amidst gracious grounds — you can easily understand why as much money was spent on the building of this home as on any other in the United States during the 1830s. The surface of the front facade is smooth, unpolished granite, while

William R. Rodman Mansion

on the sides the granite was left in its rough form. The third story dormer was not part of architect Russell Warren's original design. The small portico at the entrance is in proportion to the main portico — all blending to give a feeling of early grandeur and prosperity.

The house was built in 1833 at a cost of $75,000 for William Rotch Rodman, son of Samuel Rodman, Sr. and Elizabeth Rotch. He was director and president of the Mechanics' National Bank, a successful whaling merchant, owner of a sheep farm in Australia, part owner of a hotel in New Orleans, and one of the wealthiest men in the city when he died in 1855. He was listed in *Rich Men of Massachusetts*. Unlike his more traditional ancestors and relatives, he was a rather carefree Quaker, taking life as he found it and thoroughly enjoying it. Many a lavish party was hosted here by Mr. and Mrs. William R. Rodman.

The Honorable Abraham H. Howland bought the mansion in 1856 at auction for $25,000. Howland brought his own prestige to the mansion, having served as New Bedford's first mayor from 1847 to 1852. He was also a prosperous whaling merchant and involved in the early distillation of kerosene and coal oil. He obtained the original charter for the Wamsutta Mills, and served on several boards of directors for local companies. He was an active member of the Board of Trustees for the library and an enthusiastic volunteer fireman. Abraham H. Howland, Jr., whose career paralleled his father's, also served as mayor and was

117

equally concerned with the welfare of his city and its inhabitants. He, too, lived here for several years.

Following the Rodmans and the Howlands, who were basically whaling merchants, the next owners, Joseph F. Knowles, Thomas S. Hathaway, and Frederick Grinnell were all textile or manufacturing merchants and all from old family lines. Joseph Knowles was director and treasurer of the Acushnet Mills. Thomas S. Hathaway, with his mercantile knowledge, was active in the administration of the Acushnet Mills, Hathaway Manufacturing Company, and Page Manufacturing Company as well as the Morse Twist Drill and Machine Company, Mechanics' Bank, and the local railroad. Frederick Grinnell, not to be outdone by the previous owners, was a talented engineer with the Atlantic and Great Western Railroad. Later he obtained valuable patents on his Grinnell automatic sprinkler and Grinnell dry pipe valve. He also developed a way for fire extinguishing systems to continue to work even with frozen pipes. His inventions revolutionized fire prevention methods.

From 1919 until 1945 the house was owned by Walter H. Langshaw, an English immigrant, who worked his way up to be the president of the Dartmouth Manufacturing Company. Born in Eagley, England, in 1859 he moved at age seven with his parents to Lawrence, Massachusetts, where he worked long hours in the textile mills. In later years he moved to New Bedford and worked for Potomska Mills. Here he did such an outstanding job that, when Dartmouth Mills opened and were looking for a competent superintendent, he was offered the job in 1895. By 1900 he was a director and prime manager in the company. He was also president of the Bristol Manufacturing Company in New Bedford and held similar positions in textile mills outside New Bedford. Walter Langshaw had by merit, rather than ancestral name or inheritance, worked his way from lowly clerk to president and director of textile companies.

After settling into this prestigious mansion, he added to its interior decor with paintings from Europe, which can still be seen in the old music room. He covered several first floor walls with decorative plaster relief and closed in the windows behind the main staircase to facilitate the installation of a pipe organ. He was an accomplished organist.

After Langshaw's death in 1945, the mansion was bought by Louis Herman. It later served for a short time as a Jewish Community Center and in 1972 was purchased by the Swain School of Design.

William W. Swain was born on Nantucket Island in 1793, moved to New Bedford in 1800, and later married Lydia Russell. They had two sons, one of whom died in infancy and the other, an invalid, died at age twenty-one after completing his schooling. Being a man of wealth, loving children, and being heart-broken at the loss of his own, William Swain set up, through his will in 1858, a Free School. It was to be operated in his home for those of high character, regardless of religious or political affiliation, who wished to continue their education beyond public school but could not afford to.

Following Mrs. Swain's death, the school was opened in 1882 in the Swain home, thus fulfilling his dream of children learning and growing up in his home. The school, as a memorial to a man who lost two children but educated thousands, is now housed in the beautiful Rodman mansion and has progressed from a faculty of three to a four year accredited School of Design.

#45
William Rotch, Jr. House
396 County Street
1834
Private

The William Rotch, Jr. House is the next house on the right between Cherry and Madison Streets.

This home of William Rotch, Jr., built in 1834, is important not only for the beautifully preserved main house, but because it is one of the few such homes still retaining the formal gardens, greenhouse, carriage house, and well-maintained spacious grounds of a prominent mid-nineteenth century resident of New Bedford. The formal gardens were laid out by William's son-in-law, James Arnold*. Possibly one of the loveliest frame whaling mansions built in New Bedford, it was highly praised as such by John Quincy Adams on one of his visits to New Bedford. This Greek Revival has been owned by only three families (Rotch, Jones, Duff) and remains a private residence today. The only alteration over the years has been the addition of dormers on the third floor.

William Rotch, Jr., born on Nantucket Island in 1759, moved to New Bedford soon after the American Revolution, where he lived for sixty-three years, contributing his outstanding mercantile and business talents to the economic growth of New Bedford. Along with partner Samuel Rodman, Sr. he led the Rotch whaling enterprises in New Bedford, while his father William,

William Rotch, Jr. House

Sr. and brother Benjamin were busy running a most profitable whaling business from Dunkirk, France. It is interesting to note that William, Jr. married Elizabeth Rodman, sister of his partner Samuel Rodman, Sr., who earlier had married William, Jr.'s sister, Elizabeth Rotch. William, Jr. was one of the founders in 1825 and first president of the New Bedford Institution for Savings. As a devoted Quaker and one interested in local education, he personally contributed almost half of the money raised for the building of the Friends Academy in 1811. He served as its first treasurer and until his death in 1850 continued to serve as either treasurer or president.

William, Jr. owned two significant homes in New Bedford. The first was built in 1791 on the corner of William and Water Streets, where he lived with his first wife, Elizabeth Rotch. This house was built on the original foundation of the home of his grandfather, Joseph, who was the early dominant force in New Bedford whaling. In later years the house was given by William's daughter, Sarah Arnold, to the Port Society and moved to Johnny Cake Hill where it now serves as the Mariners' Home*. Later, through the encouragement of his second wife, Lydia Scott, he built in 1834 this more elaborate home on Madison and County Streets. Note the columned porches on three sides of the building, with the double circular stairway leading to the rear entrance.

In William's day his home was one of open hospitality to all, whether they were rich or poor, newcomer or old-timer. Along with concern for the people of his own city, he was also one of the early abolitionists. As a faithful Quaker he believed that the presence of God could be found in any individual.

Thomas H. Knowles House

#46
Thomas H. Knowles House
402 County Street
1889
Private

Cross Madison Street and the second house on the right is the Thomas H. Knowles House.

When Thomas H. Knowles graduated from Harvard, he joined his father's whaling business and later became a partner. His interests widened to cotton, and he became a director of the Acushnet Mills and Oneko Mills. He was also director of the New Bedford Gaslight Company and the Merchants' National Bank as well as a trustee of several savings banks. He was president of City Manufacturing Corporation and Bristol Manufacturing Company. Active in civic affairs, he served as an alderman, library trustee, and as Clerk of the Society in the Unitarian Church.

A later Gothic Revival, this house is an interesting study to

121

contrast with its Stick style neighbor on the south (398 County). The outstanding Gothic features are the steep intersecting peaked roof lines, the trefoil decoration of the varying hooded dormers, and the asymmetrical complexity of the whole.

Joseph Arthur Beauvais House

#47
Joseph Arthur Beauvais
    House
404 County Street
1883
Private

The next house on the right at the SE corner of County and Walnut Streets is the Joseph A. Beauvais House.

Joseph A. Beauvais was a successful and able financier and businessman. His father was captain of a packet running from New York to New Orleans and later South America. Joseph began his career in the counting rooms of his uncle, Barton Ricketson, a whaling merchant. He advanced to owning his own ships and became a broker. He was treasurer of the New Bedford Tannery Company and the American Tack Company, of which he became president. A private banker, he was president and an organizer of the Fall River Railroad Company, director of Merchants' National Bank, president of the Citizens National Bank, and an incorporator and trustee of New Bedford Five Cents Savings Bank. He was president of the New England Mutual Aid

Society, New Bedford Real Estate Association, and Weeden Manufacturing Company. He was a director of Bennett Manufacturing Company, Union Street Railroad, Grinnell Manufacturing, and many others. A Congregationalist, he was clerk and superintendent of the Sunday School.

The interesting house is a fine example of the Queen Anne style, which was New Bedford's most popular style. The main features are the projecting gables and bays, the ornate chimneys — one with incorporated dormer — a variety of wall textures, windows with differing pane sizes and emphasis, and a decoratively carved pediment.

#48

Gilbert Russell House
Dr. Edward P. Abbe House
405 County Street
c1805, 1868
Open for religious order and
day school

Across County Street, at the head of Walnut Street, on the SW corner of County and Clinton Streets is the Gilbert Russell House.

This site has been home to people who have shaped New Bedford's history through the years. In 1805 Gilbert Russell's fine home, second of three he built in New Bedford, was located here. Gilbert Russell, a successful merchant, was quiet, neat, of good character and taste. He enjoyed gardening here at his beautiful estate, where he lived for many years. He was the son of New Bedford founder Joseph Russell III. Gilbert also built the William Tallman Russell House* for his son and gave the land for the Cornelius Grinnell* and William Swain* mansions to his sons-in-law.

Russell's home was sold to William R. Rotch in 1820. Rotch died in 1860, and the house remained empty during the difficult Civil War years, until purchased by Agnes Thomas for $18,000 in 1865. Three years later, she made a tidy profit of $7,000 when she sold it to Dr. Edward P. Abbe. That same day he also obtained a $10,000 mortgage with which he totally remodeled the house to its present distinctive style. Dr. Abbe was an important person at this time in the field of medicine, active in state medical organizations. His wife was the sister of Elbridge Gerry, governor of Massachusetts and fifth Vice President of the United States.

The beautifully maintained building is one of the most spectacular of these magnificent County Street structures. Its general-

Gilbert Russell House

ly Moorish architectural feeling is a well-unified combination of massive Federal core with decorative wooden quoins, Italianate brackets, and a dramatic French mansard roof with unusual Oriental upsweep. The octagonal cupola is a fitting crown for this elegant example of New Bedford's individualistic style.

#49

Samuel W. Rodman House	Diagonally across County Street is
412 County Street	the Samuel W. Rodman House.
c1842	(On the right or east side of Coun-
Open as offices of	ty Street)
Inter-Church Council	

Samuel W. Rodman of the prominent New Bedford Quaker family was the son of William R. Rodman. Samuel W. Rodman was listed in the book *Rich Men of Massachusetts* as "having amassed the above snug sum, he sagely devotes himself to his dogs, horses, guns, and beard..."[11] Apparently sage is correct, as he lived a full ninety-two years.

    When he built this solid house, it commanded the site of the block between School and Walnut Streets. The fortress-like, rough cut, massive, granite block construction seems like a

Samuel W. Rodman House

Quaker adaptation of the usually lighter Gothic Cottage style. The sharply peaked slate roof has decorative pinnacles at the gables. The vergeboard has been removed from this rare stone Early Gothic Revival, now home to the Inter-Church Council.

#50

Grace Episcopal Church
County and School Streets
1881
Open

Continue north on County Street. Grace Episcopal Church is on the right, the NE corner of County and School Streets.

Looking at this imposing High Victorian Gothic Church of stone, you may find it difficult to appreciate its fragile beginning. In 1833, when a small group of Episcopalians wished to form their own church, they were regarded with concern and distrust, a prejudice carried over from their Anglican counterpart during the American Revolution. Also at that time most of the wealth and influence in the city was in the hands of Quakers and Unitarians.

In spite of obvious obstacles a meeting was held in Mechanic's Hall to formulate Christ's Church Parish on October 2, 1833. Their first service was led by the Reverend

125

Grace Episcopal Church

Nathaniel T. Bent. Services continued for several years in a rented building on Middle Street, where the church was affectionately called Pennyroyal after the perennial mint herb that grew on the property.

Learning that other churches, Unitarian in nature, had used names similar to Christ's Church, this first Episcopal church changed its name and was incorporated as Grace Church on March 19, 1834. Two years later a twin-towered, Gothic style, wooden church building was completed on Union Street. This building was completely renovated and the original debt paid in the 1850s during the pastorate of the Reverend Spencer M. Rice.

Miss Susan Emlen Rodman and her sister, Ellen Rodman Hathaway (Mrs. Horatio), donated in 1879 part of the Rodman lands on the corner of County and School Streets as a site for a new church building. Thanks to donations of similarily devoted parishioners and the positive influence of the Rector, The Reverend George A. Strong, the present building was completely paid for, at a cost of $47,000, by the time it was consecrated in 1882. The tower housed the first church bells in town, a donation by Stephen G. Driscoll. These 11,000 pound bells, ten in all, rang out for the first time on Christmas Eve. Ten years later a Parish House was erected adjacent to the church on land given by Horatio Hathaway.

Observe this house of worship built of granite, interspersed with rubblestone laid in red mortar, with buttresses, angles, and window jambs in brick, and accents done in Connecticut brown freestone. The varied textures of the facade, like the varied members and rectors, have united to form a cohesive and enduring building and church.

Step inside to appreciate the effect of open dark-timbered trusses in the high-ceilinged, traditional Victorian sanctuary with central altar and facing choir pews. The six stained glass windows in the chancel were given in memory of Miss Susan Emlen Rodman. Throughout the sanctuary and adjoining chapel are additional richly tinted windows, all given as memorials.

#51

Samuel Rodman, Jr. House	Next, on the right side of County
106 Spring Street	Street, on the SE corner of Coun-
1827-1828	ty and Spring Streets, is the
Open for United Way	Samuel Rodman, Jr. House.
Offices	
HABS	

Samuel Rodman, Jr. inherited a fine tradition of Quaker determination, morality, and business acumen, which he nurtured and expanded. His father, Samuel, Sr., began work in a Newport countinghouse at thirteen to support his widowed mother and six younger sisters. He developed into a leading Nantucket and later New Bedford whaling merchant and textile pioneer (see Rodman Candleworks). Samuel Junior's mother was Elizabeth Rotch, whose father, William Rotch, Sr., was a whaling king of Nantucket.

Samuel Rodman, Jr. continued the family's business successes, was a dedicated abolitionist, and was instrumental in founding the New Bedford Free Public Library and the New Bedford Port Society and Seamen's Bethel. A diarist, his detailed

127

Samuel Rodman, Jr. House

and thoughtful entries make the interested reader feel a part of his life and times. His diaries, which span 1821-1859, portray the quiet yet grand life of three generations of the Rodman Family. A true panorama of the past, they include a golden wedding, business concerns, the Civil War, children's education, in-laws, relations, and the detailed progress of building this house. All at-test to the dignity, diligence, and strong moral character of the people involved.

In 1812 he began recording temperature and weather obser-vations, which showed New Bedford's climate to be uniquely adaptable for weaving and spinning fibers. His son Thomas con-tinued the daily recordings until his death in 1905. These ninety-three years of meteorological records are now in the keeping of the United States Government. Thomas became an Episcopalian, and he and his family gave land, support, and eventually this house to the Grace Episcopal Church.

In 1940 the house was the headquarters of the New Bedford American Red Cross, which actively aided war-torn Europe. In 1942 the USO leased the building from the church and remod-eled it as a recreation center for servicemen and women. After the war, the New Bedford Community Chest and three other social agencies purchased the structure and located offices here. In 1963 a large group repaired the building, volunteering their services and materials to maintain the structure which had served so many. It continues its humanitarian role now as the head-quarters of the United Way of Greater New Bedford.

Called the plainest of New Bedford's great houses, the Samuel Rodman, Jr. House was built in 1827-1828 in the Federal style on land once part of the homestead of Abraham Russell. The house stands tall and unadorned, like an upright Quaker, with simple porticos and hip roof. Cement covers the random granite walls, originally "light Quaker brown". Gone, after many years of remodeling, are the lofty cupola lookout, several large fireplaces, the ornate trim, and an ancient elm. Much of the beauty still remains in the original moldings and stair rails, fanlighted main hall, and paneling in window embrasures and doors. Restoration is planned to save this historic treasure.

#52
James Arnold Mansion
Wamsutta Club
421 County Street
1821
Private Club

Across County Street from the Samuel Rodman, Jr. House is the James Arnold Mansion.

The building, which is now the private Wamsutta Club, was in earlier years home to two of New Bedford's well-known families, those of James Arnold and William James Rotch.

The main brick section was built in the Federal style in 1821 and set among beautiful trees and open land on what was originally the Abraham Russell farm. At that time, with County Street for all practical purposes the western end of town, large stands of trees formed the backdrop for the Arnold Mansion.

James Arnold, like his home, was an outstanding figure on the New Bedford landscape during the 1800s. He was a Quaker of great intellectual abilities, unquestionable integrity, unusual business acuity, and dedicated to the welfare of his fellowman. Born in Providence, Rhode Island, he came to New Bedford to work in William Rotch, Junior's countinghouse. He married Sarah Rotch, daughter of William, Jr., and soon became a full partner with his father-in-law, ultimately becoming one of New Bedford's merchant princes.

As an amateur botanist he collected special varities of shrubs, flowers, and trees during his trips to Europe. These he used to further beautify his formal gardens, which were interspersed with lovely landscaped paths. In the midst of these

James Arnold Mansion

gardens, which were a showplace of the town, he had a special grotto featuring stone pillars covered with sea shells brought from all over the world. Also on the eleven acres were a greenhouse, bowling alley, and stables to round out the estate of James Arnold, one of the millionaires of New Bedford.

In spite of his great wealth Arnold felt a deep concern for those less fortunate than himself. Monies and help were given freely from this house on the hill to the needy of New Bedford. He was also one of the early abolitionists and gave financial and physical support to slaves during the years of the Underground Railroad, which was especially active in the city.

Through his will he left $100,000 to the Union for Good Works to be used for the deserving poor. He was also a generous benefactor of the Association for the Relief of Aged Women, and left $6,000 for the work of the Bethel through the New Bedford Port Society, of which he had been one of the early presidents. He left $100,000 to Harvard to be used for advancement of horticulture. This proved to be the financial beginning for the now famous Arnold Arboretum, which has a specie of every shrub and tree that can endure the Massachusetts climate. His influence continued far beyond his mortal years.

Upon Arnold's death the house was left to his nephew, William James Rotch*, who at that time was living in the Gothic Cottage at 19 Irving Street. William moved with his second wife, Clara Morgan, and seven children to this home in 1872. At that time William added the third story and the Second Empire Period mansard roof. Over the years other additions have been made. However, the second and third floor of the main building remain in their original form.

William J. Rotch lived on in the mansion until his death in 1893, and his widow, Clara, remained another twenty-six years. Clara was the last person to use the mansion as a private home, for after her death in 1919 it was bought by the Wamsutta Club. Today this lively historic mansion, still surrounded by gracious lawns, continues as home to the well-known Wamsutta Club.

#53

First Unitarian Church	From County Street turn right on
Union and Eighth Streets	Union Street and go one block.
1838	The Unitarian Church is on the
Open for church services	left, the NW corner of Union and
office open daily	Eighth Streets.

Here in this New England seaport city stands a fortress to man's faith. Looking as though it would be at home among the castles of medieval England, this rough-cut stone, Early Gothic Revival church traces its history back to 1708. At that time the first church was built in Acushnet in the township of Dartmouth, which included today's New Bedford. This church is unusual in that through its history it embraced Congregationalists, Baptists, Quakers, and Unitarians among its membership.

The first church, built in Acushnet at the head of the river, was known as the First Congregational Society. Its first minister, the Reverend Samuel Hunt, was assigned by the Puritan-minded General Court of the Massachusetts Bay Colony. In those early days there were only sixteen Puritan families in the area, while the majority of the colonists were Quakers and Baptists, who saw no reason to support a church foreign to their own beliefs. The Reverend Hunt showed unusual understanding for both groups and did much to minimize the differences. Nevertheless, matters came to a head in 1722 when Baptist and Quaker oriented town officials refused to collect taxes for the support of the Puritan church and were imprisoned. The townspeople readily raised

the name was officially changed to the First Unitarian Church in New Bedford.

The present church was completed in 1838 on land purchased from William Rotch, Jr. for $6000. Architects of this imposing ediface were Russell Warren and Alexander Jackson Davis. The church is ecumenical in its atmosphere. As you enter the large three-aisle Gothic hall, notice banners representing many of the religions of the world. At the front of the church is a beautiful mosaic window, designed by Frederick Wilson and done in the studio of Louis C. Tiffany. This is the largest such Tiffany window in existence. The music is enhanced by a Flentrop organ.

Dr. Dana McLean, President of the Unitarian Universalist Association, said at the re-dedication service of the building in 1967, "Here let no man be a stranger, that in our sharing we may find understanding, fulfillment and joy."[12]

#54

Nathan and Polly Johnson Properties	Go one block east on Union Street and turn right on Seventh Street. After crossing Spring Street, you can see the Johnson Properties on the right side starting at the corner from #17 through #23. Note the present Friends Meeting House diagonally across on Spring Street.
17-23 Seventh Street	
c1785	
Private	

Nathan Johnson, a well known Black in New Bedford during the 1800s, owned the properties from 17 through 23 Seventh Street. He and his wife, Polly, lived at number 17-19 and together ran a confectionary business on the site of number 21. The store was an active front for the Underground Railroad. The Johnsons were close friends of Frederick Douglass, speaker, writer, and nationally known Black anti-slavery leader, who lived for a time with the Johnsons. In fact, it was Nathan Johnson who first met the penniless Douglass when he arrived in town on the stage. Johnson paid his fare and took him to his home. Then, from his knowledge of literature, he gave this runaway-slave the name Frederick Douglass.

The house on the corner, number 17-19, was the first Friends Meeting House originally built on Spring Street in 1785. When the Society of Friends needed a new, larger meetinghouse

134

Nathan and Polly Johnson properties

the old one was bought in 1821 for $270.75, probably by William Rotch, Jr., and given to the Johnsons. The building which became their home was moved here to Seventh Street to land then owned by Samuel Rodman, Sr. Eight years later Charles W. Morgan, son-in-law of Samuel Rodman, Sr., sold the property to Nathan and Polly Johnson for $596. The austere, Federal style building served in later years as Mrs. Waite's School, then a private residence and dentist office, was severely damaged by fire in 1934, and is now used as apartments.

Giving his wife power of attorney, Nathan Johnson left New Bedford for California in 1849. After her death in 1871 he returned to the city to receive his share of her inheritance and remained here until his death in 1880.

It is interesting to note that the Friends Society organized a branch of the Anti-Slavery Society as early as 1834, and many of their members were very active in the Underground Railroad. Thus it seems only fitting that their old meetinghouse should have been sold to Nathan Johnson, himself a Black and strong supporter of the abolitionist movement.

George Howland, Sr. House

#55
George Howland, Sr. House
245 Walnut Street
1812
Private apartments

Continue south on Seventh Street, crossing School Street, to Walnut Street. The George Howland, Sr. House is on the left, the NE corner of Walnut and Seventh Streets.

George Howland, Sr. built this suitably stately Federal mansion in 1812. He was an outstanding figure at the time of New Bedford's prime, one of her first millionaires. A leading whale shipowner and merchant, he was a trustee of the Friends Academy and the first president of the Bedford Commercial Bank, a position he held for thirty-six years until his death. His early career began in the counting rooms of William Rotch, Jr.,* where he achieved success even before he "came of age".

George Howland, Sr. called "one of nature's strong men"[13] by historian Daniel Ricketson, was a true Quaker in belief and behavior. He had an innate military-like ability which he applied with great success to his mercantile interests.

From the then commanding position of this house, George and his bride Susan were able to watch their new ship, *George and Susan,* launched on her career which would nearly span the century. Now the Federal mansion is barely discernable. Victorian modifications in Italianate and Queen Anne styles have completely changed the appearance.

Jireh Swift, Jr. House

#56

Jireh Swift, Jr. House
96 Madison Street
1865
Private

Turn right on Walnut Street and go to County Street. Turn left for one block to Madison Street and turn right. The Jireh Swift, Jr. House is the first one on the left side of the street.

Jireh Swift, Jr., born in 1809, was the seventh generation to descend from William Swift of Watertown in 1634 and the fifth to be named Jireh. He was a highly reputed and honorable merchant and banker, considered a captain of industry. A Unitarian and prominent in New Bedford community activities, he was honored to have a school named for him.

Jireh Swift VI continued in this tradition. Educated at the Friends Academy and Harvard, he became an international merchant and cotton broker, with much of his activity centered in Brazil. He was president of the New Bedford Five Cents Savings Bank, an alderman, and a library trustee. His wife was also prominent in civic work. Her portrait was so lovely it was given by the artist to the Padanaram Library.

The four square, handsome house is of the Italian Villa style with the cupola, heavy brackets, and architraves crowning the windows. The delightful Italianate round-arched door is highlighted by rope molding, distinctive of New Bedford and appropriately reflecting her nautical past and present. The house reveals Renaissance Revival influences in the more simple, symmetrical exterior and the string course under the third floor windows. The corner pilasters are Greek Revival. The house is a splendid example of affluent post Industrial Revolution New Bedford and the successful combination of architectural styles.

Benjamin Anthony House

#57
Benjamin Anthony House
98 Madison Street
1889
Private

The next house, on the same side of the street, is the Benjamin Anthony House at number 98.

Benjamin Anthony was the financial guide of the *Standard,* a newspaper which his father, Edmond Anthony, founded. He followed his father to become the *Standard*'s president. His son, Benjamin Harris Anthony, succeeded him as treasurer. Benjamin Anthony was a director of the New Bedford Co-operative Bank and the Acushnet Co-operative Bank. A Methodist, he was a trustee, treasurer, and Sunday School librarian for twenty-five years.

The house is an interesting combination of Shingle style, reminiscent of the Newport mansions, and Queen Anne style. The projecting gables, dormers, and turrets, the variety of exterior finishes, the multiple size panes within one window are the Queen Anne features massed within the more unified, bulging effect of the Shingle style.

Mrs. Elizabeth G. Leonard House (Andrew G. Pierce, Jr. House)

#58
Mrs. Elizabeth G. Leonard
Andrew G. Pierce, Jr.
  House
99 Madison Street
1881
Private

The Andrew G. Pierce, Jr. House is across the street at number 99 on the NE corner of Madison and Orchard Streets.

Andrew G. Pierce, Jr. faced the difficult challenge of following his outstanding father and succeeded admirably. Andrew G. Pierce, Sr., New Bedford's ninth mayor, was handsome, and kind as well as a great textile leader, banker, and captain of many industries.

Andrew G. Pierce, Jr. worked his way up through the Wamsutta Mills after attending MIT. He became president and board chairman of the American Woolen Company, was president of Pairpoint Glass Corporation for twenty-seven years, and was president of Pierce Manufacturing Company, Grinnell Mill, and Consolidated Textile Corporation of New York. He was a director of the First National Bank of Boston and the First National Bank of New Bedford. He was an influential developer of cotton manufacturing. At the height of his career New Bedford was producing "a mile of cloth a minute"[14] in its mills. This modest Yankee, who could trace his ancestry to William the Conqueror, was also known as the wool king. In 1929, he received an annual salary of $200,000 as president of American Woolen. Mrs. Andrew G. Pierce, Jr. was a civic leader with an early interest in women's role in politics.

This fine Queen Anne style house, originally owned by Mrs. Elizabeth G. Leonard, features projecting gables, a conical turret, and arched spindle work on the front porch. The massive chimneys and variety of wall surfaces further mark the Queen Anne style, with the transition to Shingle style evident in the more unified, seemingly bulging mass of the overall design. Recently rescued by WHALE*, the house is being rehabilitated.

#59
Captain Henry Taber House
115 Orchard Street
c1847
Private offices
HABS

The Captain Henry Taber House is on the far side of Orchard almost at the head of Madison Street.

Captain Henry Taber's story is typical of the successful sea captains of New Bedford. At fourteen he adventured to sea as a cabin boy on his first voyage with his Uncle John Wood, who was master of the *George and Susan,* owned by George Howland, Sr.* He worked his way up, with more responsibility on each long voyage, until he gained command. Over the next fifteen years he captained four ships: *Orbit, Boston, Experiment,* and *Helen.*

Captain Taber came in from the sea to become a ships' chandler and grocer and to run a packet line. With the upsurge in whaling he added to his packet line, which sailed between New Bedford and Boston, built freight schooners, and expanded to other related fields of business. Captain Taber was a member of the state legislature, president of a marine insurance company, and director of the National Bank of Commerce.

The tall stately residence seems almost Federal but is Greek Revival with the gable end perpendicular to the street. The

Captain Henry Taber House

delicately styled portico is supported by Corinthian columns with intricate fan and side lights at the front entrance. The side ell repeats the columns and balustrades of the portico. At corners and roof line the wide pilasters and entablature of the Greek Revival style add the unifying decorative detail.

#60
William J. Rotch Gothic
   Cottage
19 Irving Street
1846
Private

Turn right on Orchard Street, then left on Maple Street, and go one block to Irving Street. The William J. Rotch Gothic Cottage is on the left, the SW corner of Maple and Irving Streets.

This imposing Early Gothic Revival Cottage is one of the most unusual and interesting homes in New Bedford. The lines of the house seem to draw your eyes upward, indicating an atmosphere of strength, high purpose, and gracious living. Notice the elaborate, carved fretwork under the steeply angled eaves, the pinnacle dramatically piercing the gable over the front entrance, the ship-lap wood or flat board facade, and the tall narrow double windows with triangular glass panes and wood molding. It is necessary to absorb all the varieties of design to

William J. Rotch Gothic Cottage

truly appreciate this classic in Gothic Cottage architecture, designed by Alexander Jackson Davis and listed in A. J. Downing's, *The Architecture of Country Houses,* 1850.

William James Rotch, born in 1819, married Emily Morgan, daughter of Charles W. Morgan, original owner of the famous whaling ship now on display at Mystic, Connecticut. When William and Emily were honeymooning in New York's Hudson River region, they became fascinated with Gothic style cottages. Shortly afterward, they surprised traditional-minded New Bedford with their own Gothic cottage, built here in 1846 on land deeded to William by his grandfather, William Rotch, Jr., for one dollar plus his love and good will.

The cottage, surrounded by well-maintained rolling lawns, circular drive, and stables, faced Orchard Street before Irving or Maple Streets were laid out. As William's family grew, he found it necessary to hire architect William Ralph Emerson to build an addition to the house in keeping with the Gothic Revival design.

William J. Rotch, like his home, was a unique figure in town. At age thirty-three he was the second mayor of the city. During his unusually productive and varied lifetime he was on the board of directors of almost every corporation in town. He was closely associated with his brother, Benjamin S., in many business enterprises. He was on Governor Clifford's military staff, served two terms in the Massachusetts Legislature 1848-1850, and for forty-two years was president and/or treasurer of the Friends Academy. He was President of the Howland Mills Corporation and the Rotch Wharf Company and Vice President of the New Bedford Institution for Savings. He was also one of the founders of the Republican Party in Southeastern Massachusetts. It is hard to imagine a busier man in town than William J. Rotch. Along with other members of his family, he was also a devoted abolitionist and concerned with the welfare of the less fortunate. He was an outstanding orator, always courteous and dignified, and well liked by his fellowman.

His wife Emily died following the birth of their eighth child in 1861. Five years later William married her sister, Clara. In 1872 they moved their large family into the mansion on County Street left to William by his uncle, James Arnold*. Here their only child, Mary R. Rotch, was born.

The Gothic Cottage was rented to William Wallace Crapo, lawyer, politician, state representative, United States Congressman, orator, president of local cotton mills and banks — a man who faithfully served his city, state, and country for almost a century. In 1879 William J. Rotch's son Morgan married and asked the Crapos to move, so that he could return to his childhood home. Like his father, he served as mayor of New Bedford and was active in many of the business enterprises in the city, having a special talent as a financier. He extended Irving and Maple Streets through his property, moved the main house to the southwest corner of Irving and Maple Streets, moved the addition to 112 Cottage Street where it now stands, and sold some of the property as house lots.

In 1928 Morgan's widow, Josephine, sold the house to Henry H. Crapo, who had lived here as a boy. In 1945 Henry Crapo's niece, Catherine, and her husband, John M. Bullard, nephew of Morgan Rotch, moved into this home of common ancestral bonds. Today the home is owned by their grandson, John K. Bullard, who, in the tradition of the Rotch family, is still concerned with the welfare of New Bedford.

As the knowledge and enthusiasm of the first Joseph Rotch was the driving force behind the whaling industry in 1765, so generations later John K. Bullard has been the driving force behind the historic preservation and economic revival of the waterfront area. Mr. Bullard, with his professional training in architecture and love for his community, has inspired separate historic, economic, and city groups to unite in a successful reawakening of New Bedford through sound economic, architectural, and historic rehabilitation. The spirit of the Rotch family continues to be felt in New Bedford.

Edward S. Taber House

#61

Edward S. Taber House
143 Cottage Street
1857
Private Apartments

Continue on Maple Street to Cottage Street and turn right. Go two blocks north on Cottage Street. After you cross Arnold Street the Edward S. Taber House is the second on the left. Notice the interesting variety of architectural styles — Queen Anne, Stick, Shingle, Italianate — as you drive down Cottage Street.

Born into one of the oldest families in New Bedford, Edward Smith Taber graduated from Friends Academy and went to work for his father as a pump and block maker. Next he clerked for George Howland the whaling merchant with interests in fitting out whalers, oil manufacturing, and other whaling related businesses. After the Civil War and the decline of whaling, Edward Taber worked with steam engines in Providence and tried his own business, which was not successful. He returned to New Bedford to head the struggling Morse Twist Drill Company, which grew substantially under his leadership. He became president and director of the First National Bank and a trustee for the

New Bedford Institution for Savings.

Edward Taber's Italianate Villa style house stands staunchly among its interesting Queen Anne neighbors at 140 and 152 Cottage Street. The property was purchased by Taber's bride-to-be, Emily H. Allen, from James Arnold*. The impressive structure is sheathed in ship-lap siding, with the front facade highlighted by the columned portico and surmounting projecting set of windows. Extended lintels decorate the windows, while brackets and dentils complete the overhanging roof line and are repeated in the portico, cupola, and small crowning gable.

The Octagon

#62
The Octagon
347 Union Street
1848
Private

Continue on Cottage Street to Union Street. The Octagon is on the left, the NW corner.

Orson S. Fowler strongly advocated octagonal houses for healthy living. He felt the air circulation was superior and the floor plan more efficient. Fowler was a phrenologist who wrote about health, happiness, and sex. He wrote A Home for All, or the Gravel Wall and Octagon Mode of Building from which this and most American octagons were built. John F. Vinal, a housewright, built the house and sold it to Captain Fordyce Dennis Haskell, master of the ship, *Mercury*.

#63
Union Street Italian Villa Style Houses
On Union Street between Orchard and Cottage Streets
1851-1858
Private

Turn right on Union Street and the Italian Villa Style Houses are on the right side of Union starting with the corner house No. 350 and going east on Union Street through No. 324. The Edward Haskell House at 345 Union Street is across the street on the NE corner of Cottage and Union Streets.

The five Italianate houses on the south side of Union Street were built on some of the first house lots sold by James Arnold* from his estate's magnificent gardens. It is interesting to note the similarities in the houses, though each is an individual with distinct features. All are four square, with large projecting gables in the middle of the facades, and crowned by cupolas.

Hosea M. Knowlton House
350 Union Street, c1852, Private
This house was built by whaling merchant Barnabas S. Perkins and later owned by Hosea M. Knowlton. Mr. Knowlton

Hosea M. Knowlton House

was the prosecutor of the Lizzie Borden murder trial and later the state's attorney general. The house has many of the Italian Villa style features, with the plain window treatment a notable exception.

Deacon Edward S. Cannon House
342 Union Street, c1858, Offices
Deacon Cannon was a dedicated worker for the North Congregational Church. He initiated a missionary movement in the western section of the city, which culminated in the building of a small chapel at the corner of Kempton and Rockdale Avenues, known as Cannonville Chapel. It and the surrounding area were named in his honor.

A fine example of Italian Villa style, the house has more intricate detail in the entablature near the roof line. Dormers pierce the hip roof, and the window treatment is more conservative.

Deacon Edward S. Cannon House

Tilson Bourne Denham House
334 Union Street, 1857, Apartments and offices
Tilson Bourne Denham was prominent in New Bedford city politics and a member of the state legislature. A prosperous baker and whale ship supplier, Denham was also concerned with military affairs and interested in the Fire Department. His interest in horticulture, particularly fruits and vegetables, led to his supplying hospitals and the front lines during the Civil War with

147

Tilson Bourne Denham House

welcome preserves and wine. Denham descended from a Pilgrim founder and member of Governor Bradford's Council. His son Thomas followed him as a legislator, and son Edward was an historian and writer of note.

The house seems simpler than its neighbors, due to the bracketed roofs being parallel to the street and unbroken by projections.

James Hammett House
330 Union Street, c1856, Apartments and offices

James Hammett, a daily commuter to his brokerage office in Boston, built this house about 1856. It was later owned by

James Hammett House

Thomas Brownell Wilcox, owner of a fruit and grocery concern and treasurer and director of the New Bedford Glass Company.

The Italianate roof line dominates all facades of the house which has flush boarding on the front.

Nehemiah Waterman House
324 Union Street, 1856, Apartment and offices

A successful auctioneer, Nehemiah Waterman also acted as an amateur ventriloquist and magician. Several features distinguish this home from its neighbors: the intersecting gable roof, projecting rear ell, and enclosed balcony on the front facade.

Nehemiah Waterman House

Edward Haskell House
345 Union Street, 1868, Offices

Though not of the original five built on Arnold land, the Haskell mansion is architecturally appropriate for the neighborhood. The large square Italianate mass has ship-lap siding, projecting dormers, and an elaborate, bracketed, French mansard roof line complete with ornamental balustrades. The

Edward Haskell House

impressive entrance is crowned by an enclosed balcony, and the windows have a variety of caps. Once an intricate iron fence surrounded landscaped gardens, a greenhouse, an aviary, and a coach house. Edward Haskell had a prosperous dry goods business and was active in the North Congregational Church, where he was a Superintendent of the Sabbath School. Unaccountably, in 1882 he killed himself by putting a bullet through his brain.

#64
Jireh Perry House
Masonic Temple
435 County Street
c1839
Open as Masonic Temple

Continue east on Union Street. The Jireh Perry House is on the left, the NW corner of Union and County Streets.

Jireh Perry was a prosperous whaling merchant and incorporator of the Wamsutta Mills. He built his brick home dur-

Jireh Perry House

ing a conservative period of wealth and transition, combining late Federal with Greek Revival. It remained in his family until about the turn of the century when it housed the Wamsutta Club*. It has been added to considerably since then.

CLARK'S POINT AREA

Directions for #'s 65-70 relate to the City of New Bedford map on p. viii-ix

#65
East Beach and Hurricane
  Barrier Access
East Rodney French
  Boulevard
Open all year, no fee,
  facilities open summer
  only

HURRICANE BARRIER AC-CESS: (see #23) Continue east to foot of Union Street. Turn right onto J.F. Kennedy Highway (Route 18). After you enter the highway, keep left at fork. Continue to end of highway, turn left and go to Front Street. Turn right and go to Gifford Street and turn left. Park at the end of Gifford to walk out on the Hurricane Barrier.

East Beach: Return on Gifford Street to Morton Court and turn

151

left. Continue to Cove Street and turn left. At the Hurricane Barrier wall, Cove Street bears right and becomes East Rodney French Boulevard. A 1½ mile scenic drive leads to East Beach. Facilities: lifeguards, parking, showers, rest rooms, concession stand, playground.

East Beach on Buzzards Bay is New Bedford's longest sandy beach and provides protected swimming in summer and beach walking and ocean gazing all year.

Looking back toward the city you can see the Hurricane Barrier* — especially pretty at twilight or nightfall, with the navigational aid lights and those of Fairhaven sparkling across the wide outer harbor. Near at hand, directly across, is Butler's Flats Light,* still a warm beacon to returning men and women of the sea. Looking out to sea, your eye follows the skyline of Fairhaven's shores to the open outer harbor, Fort Taber,* and Buzzards Bay, leading to the open sea.

#66
Butler's Flats Light
Off East Beach

Butler's Flats Light can be seen from East Beach and the drive along East Rodney French Boulevard.

Butler's Flats Light still glows its welcome to men coming home from the Banks. It stands as a tribute to a group of private citizens who changed the mind of the United States Coast Guard. The Coast Guard was flooded with protests when plans to place a new beacon on the Hurricane Barrier* and destroy this light were announced. The Coast .Guard heeded the pleas and saved the light, though it was deactivated in 1978 and a new beacon was placed on the barrier for superior navigational aid. As a result of the work of caring citizens, the light is now owned by the city and privately maintained by some of those who saved it.

The light was constructed in 1898 for $34,000 by F. Hopkinson Smith, a versatile individual who was also noted as an author, painter, and ironwork expert. Smith is credited with building the breakwaters at Block Island, the seawall around Governor's Island, New York, the foundation for the Statue of Liberty, and

East Beach and Butler's Flats Light

the Race Rock Lighthouse off New London.

Construction was a challenge, as the light had no natural rock foundation. A thirty-five foot diameter cylinder was filled with stone and concrete, and the light built above. Fifty-three feet above mean low level tide, the light could be seen for five miles or more. Living quarters eighteen feet in diameter housed the lightkeepers, with the wide balcony providing the only walking exercise space.

Three generations of Captain Bakers have devotedly tended Butler's Flats Light. Captain Amos Baker, a retired whaler, was keeper of the old light on Clark's Point. He became the first keeper of Butler's Flats and was succeeded by his son, Captain Amos Baker, Jr., once master of the bark *A. R. Tucker*. In 1897 Grover Cleveland visited the light and signed the guest book. Captain Charlie Baker took over from his father in 1912 and began his tenure which would be the last civilian watch. In 1942 the Coast Guard manned the light, ending the eighty-two years of service by the Bakers.

1978 saw the light returned to a civilian aid to navigation, with Port Support of New Bedford, a private group, maintaining the light. This historic harbor marker is another New Bedford treasure cooperatively and effectively preserved.

#67

Fort Taber
Clark's Point
1860
Open seasonally, no fee,
   donations accepted
NRHP

Follow East Rodney French
Boulevard to the tip of Clark's
Point. Enter Fort Rodney. Drive
straight ahead, staying next to the
shore line. Follow the road
around to Fort Taber.

Enter through the sally port of this well-preserved and partially restored Civil War fort; explore the officers' and enlisted men's quarters on the inland side and the gun emplacements on the bay side; climb the two flights of circular granite stairs to the earth covered summit, and sense the paradoxical feeling of standing atop a military fortification while drinking in the beauty and peacefulness of Buzzards Bay with the Elizabeth Islands in view and Martha's Vineyard on the horizon.

Clark's Point, where Fort Taber now stands, has long served as guardian to the harbor and to the city of New Bedford. Here over the years have been important military and navigational installations.

The first coastal installations were built here, as earthworks, during the American Revolution to protect the town from British attack. Then in 1818 the United States Board of Engineers drew up a plan for coastal defense — the first such plan done entirely by American-born engineers. The plan called for a defense system on Clark's Point. In 1846 Major Richard Delafield, known as the father of American Coastal Defense, and ironically Captain Robert E. Lee, who would soon lead the Confederacy against the Union, collaborated on a design for what would become Fort Taber.

The building of Fort Taber, named for the Honorable Isaac C. Taber, mayor of New Bedford during the Civil War, began in 1860. For a period of time Captain Henry M. Robert, who later wrote *Robert's Rules of Order,* was in charge of the construction. It was designed to have three tiers of gun mounts instead of its present two tiers. However, by 1869 the mode of warfare had so changed — with improved armaments, steam power, and iron clad ships — that this type of fortification was no longer adequate, and work was stopped.

In 1892 this hexagonal fort was turned over to the city for use as a park, only to be reclaimed six years later during the Spanish-American War. At that time the observation tower, housing a range finder, was built on the western corner. The east

Fort Taber

bastions were converted to mining casemates for control of mines in the harbor, and a searchlight unit was installed. The fort was reactivated for the last time during World War I.

During the American Revolution the point became important as a navigational aid for mariners. The town merchants financed the first lighthouse in 1797 to help guide their ships safely into port. Though the lighthouse burned a year later, it was quickly replaced and turned over to the federal government in 1800. Once again in 1804 fire took its toll. This time the government rebuilt with rubblestone. The light served for years as a friendly guide to the ocean-weary sailors. After Fort Taber was built the light was moved to the northeast corner of the fort in 1869. Again fire struck, destroying the light in 1965. It has since been replaced, though it is now inoperative. The copper cupola atop the present light is all that remains of the earlier one. You can visit the light and, by climbing to the top, have a magnificent view of the harbor and bay.

To add to your appreciation of the historic value of this fort, which has never been fired on by an enemy, visit the Visitor's Center for an audio-visual presentation and an historic photographic exhibit.

#68

Hazelwood Park
West Rodney French
  Boulevard
Open all year, no fee

Exit from Fort Rodman and turn left on West Rodney French Boulevard. Follow the Boulevard around Clark's Point and along Clark's Cove to Hazelwood Park, which will be on the right just after Lucas Street. Facilities: picnicking, lawn bowling, tennis, basketball, tot playground, fields, rest rooms, parking.

From here you can watch waves breaking on the shore and the sun setting over South Dartmouth across the cove, with the last rays reflecting on windows of mills that have long served the economy of the city. Hazelwood Park is a green oasis of twenty-three acres, offering quiet sanctuary and free recreation to all.

The trees of the George Washington Memorial Grove were planted in 1932 on the 200th anniversary of his birth by the New Bedford Daughters of the American Revolution.

The Gothic cottage houses park facilities, surrounded by an extensive tot playground, open lawns, lighted tennis courts, an unusual bowling green, and many benches from which to enjoy the vista of Clark's Cove.

#69

West Beach
West Rodney French
  Boulevard
Open all year, no fee,
  facilities, summer only

West Beach is across from Hazelwood Park. Facilities: lifeguards, bathhouse, rest rooms, pavilion, concession stands, boat launching, limited parking.

The open sandy beach provides protected swimming on lovely Clark's Cove. The southern section is rocky, a pretty setting to stroll along and enjoy the beautiful view of the cove.

#70

Buttonwood Park
Rockdale Avenue and
  Hawthorn Street
Open all year, no entrance
  fee

Follow West Rodney French Boulevard north to Cove Road (at Brightman Square just past Grit Street) and turn left. Bearing left, follow the Hurricane Barrier

along Cove Road to Rockdale
Ave. (at "V" in road, just before
Barrier gate and after Orchard
Street). Bear right onto Rockdale
Ave. and follow it to Buttonwood
Park on the left. Facilities: zoo,
greenhouses, refreshment stand,
rest rooms, tennis, ball fields,
paddleboats, train rides, ice
skating, fishing, picnicking, parking.

This excellent, many-faceted park is designed for all ages
and interests, from the lethargic to the energetic. Organized
athletic teams play in one area, while another section has extensive, colorful playground equipment. Nearby are lighted tennis
courts, inviting greenhouses, an open air stage, tree-lined drives
and walks, a fishing pond, and an extensive zoo in a natural setting. The park also features, for a small fee, train and pad-
dleboat rides.

Several memorials are found throughout the park, the
largest capped by a strong visaged man and dedicated to New
Bedford's whalemen and their successors.

As you approach the zoo, you are greeted by a black bear in
a natural looking stone den, unobtrusively fenced. Beyond, in the
enclosed area, the main zoo has thirty-five different kinds of
animals including naturally entertaining harbor seals, a special
fox exhibit, and a petting zoo. Buffalo, raccoons, leopards,
wolves, an elephant, llamas, and deer are some of the other
species found here.

The ninety-three acres of wooded and open expanses are
well used and beautifully maintained.

NORTH BEDFORD HISTORIC DISTRICT

When owned by the Kempton family, the land was open and
settlement sparse, but this changed with the early 1800s. It
developed well after the Revolution when the skilled artisans,
needed by the growth of whaling and later the development of industry, built their homes here in the North Bedford District. At
this same time, merchants and sea captains were building their
mansions in the County Street District. All the fascinating
varieties of Revivalism architecture can be found here in dense

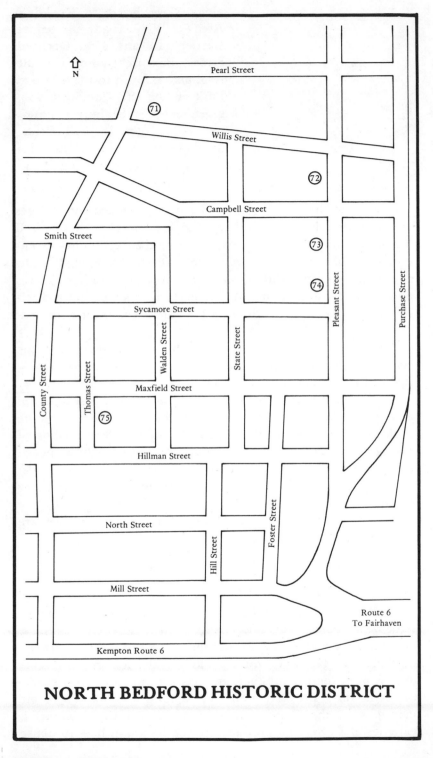

NORTH BEDFORD HISTORIC DISTRICT

N

Pearl Street

71

Willis Street

72

Campbell Street

Smith Street

73

74

Pleasant Street

Purchase Street

Sycamore Street

Walden Street

State Street

County Street

Thomas Street

Maxfield Street

75

Hillman Street

North Street

Hill Street

Foster Street

Mill Street

Route 6
To Fairhaven

Kempton Route 6

profusion, and it is interesting to compare them with those of the County Street District. The nineteenth century prevails in this center of middle class America, nearly undisturbed by the twentieth century.

#71

John Avery Parker Wing	Follow Rockdale Avenue north to Route 6 or Kempton Street and turn right. Follow Kempton Street back toward the river. Turn left on County Street and go eight blocks to Willis Street. Turn right on Willis. The John Avery Parker house will be the second house on the left.
53 Willis Street	
1834	
Private	

As you look at this unusually sturdy, stone Greek Revival home, in your imagination supply the missing huge estate of which this was a small part. Constructed of granite, the main central core was flanked by wings on either side. What remains today is one of those wings. The woodwork was all mahogany, the door knobs were of silver, and the quality so great that doors closed with the solid authority of a bank vault. The "palace" was intriguing for its architecture as well as its builder, one of New Bedford's first millionaires, John Avery Parker, and a later owner, textile pioneer Thomas Bennett, Jr.

Historian Philip F. Purrington said, "John Avery Parker responded to difficulty as a stimulus."[15] He had failed so badly in his business in Westport that in 1803 town officials told him to leave, as they didn't want to have to support his family as paupers. From this inauspicious beginning, he became a shipbuilder and fitter, owner and manager of cotton mills, owner of iron mills, first president of the Merchants National Bank, incorporator of the Old Colony Railroad, bank director, and state representative and senator. Shrewd and energetic, he was a great agent of change, a real force in the development and enrichment of New Bedford. Parker was a persistent fighter for free public education. He organized and commanded a company to defend New Bedford during the War of 1812. Though he lived in grandeur, John Avery Parker retained the simple life and was an active supporter of his Congregational church.

Thomas Bennett, Jr. was a fitting successor to Parker, as the next owner of the mansion, which he purchased about 1864.

159

John Avery Parker Wing

When whaling was at its peak, he approached Joseph Grinnell*, a leading New Bedford entrepeneur, with plans to build a cotton mill. Thus began the Wamsutta Mills, which became one of the largest and most respected cotton manufacturers in the world. Bennett also supervised the mills and designed the original building plus later additions, including the first brick mill, Wamsutta Number 4, on Acushnet Avenue.

The palace, built in 1834 at a cost of $100,000, was described by noted American architect Joy Wheeler Dow as the "finest example of transitional architecture extant in the United States."[16] It was designed by Russell Warren. Dow considered it Warren's finest work and tried valiantly to save it. Dow urged the city to use the mansion as a museum, but the greater part of it was demolished in 1902.

John Avery Parker Mansion

The remaining section of cut stone, with Greek Ionic pillars, has six carved fireplaces still in use. The outside lamps, from the old Police Station, were a gift to New Bedford Police Chief Henry Mason when he lived here.

#72

Charles Russell House
Hetty Green Residence
1061 Pleasant Street
1830
Private convent

Continue down Willis Street two blocks to Pleasant Street and turn right; go one block to Campbell Street. The Charles Russell House is on the right, the NW corner of Campbell and Pleasant Streets.

This impressive stone combination of Federal and Greek Revival was built by Charles Russell*, son of Seth Russell, Sr.* and later was the home of the infamous "Witch of Wall Street",[17] Hetty Green. In 1873 the house served as the city's first hospital, St. Joseph's, and is now a convent.

Hetty Green was the natural product of her bizarre upbringing. She could read and understand the financial pages at the age of six. These she read to her grandfather, with whom she

Charles Russell House (Hetty Green)

lived in overstated frugality in his bachelor-oriented home. She married Edward Henry Green, and the couple was considered wealthy even by Wall Street standards. She craftily and sometimes unscrupulously parlayed her large inheritance into a huge fortune, dropping her husband along the way. She valued frugality to the exclusion of rationality. She amassed a staggering fortune in the world of finance, real estate, and Wall Street, yet lived in a cheap, cold-water flat and denied her children's basic physical and medical needs. Her son Colonel E.H.R. Green, who lost a leg from his Mother's penuriousness, lived very differently and equally bizarrely.

The house is a combination of architectural periods. A tall, stately Federal, it has a hip roof and corner chimneys. The Greek Revival features are the granite walls and classical porticos supported by Doric columns.

#73
Thomas C. Lothrop House
Knights of Columbus Hall
1049 Pleasant Street
c1835
Open as Knights of Columbus Hall

The Thomas C. Lothrop House is across Campbell Street from the Charles Russell House on the SW corner of Pleasant and Campbell Streets.

The house was originally built about 1835 by Thomas Lothrop. Lothrop had a mercantile business, was superintendent

Thomas C. Lothrop House

of a Wareham ironworks, and was the son-in-law of John Avery Parker*. At the time of the Civil War the house was owned by Anna E. Hadley, whose husband was a prosperous whaling merchant and co-organizer of New Bedford's first petroleum refinery. During this time it was remodeled to its present French Second Empire style, recognizable by the dominating mansard roof and projections and the Italianate fluted classical columns and bracketed cupola. It is erroneously labeled the William F. Dow house.

The house late in 1913 was used as a hospital, the Derby Hospital named for its owner Dr. Charles A. Derby. About ten years later it became the Knights of Columbus Hall.

#74

State Armory	The Armory is adjacent to the
5 Sycamore Street	Lothrop House, on the NW cor-
1904	ner of Sycamore and Pleasant
Open all year, no fee	Streets.

This massive granite fortress, of ancient Gothic design, appropriately houses the National Guard. The Armory is one of the two remaining as such in Massachusetts. Guard units have been called from New Bedford throughout history, serving in Vietnam, and most recently to aid civilians during the Blizzard of 1978.

State Armory

Within the stone bastion is Memorial Hall, dedicated on the bicentennial to all veterans in the greater New Bedford area. It is a memorial to their participation and sacrifice in defense of their country's freedom. The hall is a center of military, social, and civic activities and open daily. Memorial flags and plaques were presented by veteran and service organizations and private individuals and are the focus of the hall. Included among the twenty-seven flags are a Betsey Ross Flag, a Bicentennial Flag, flags of organizations and other nations, as well as the American Flag.

#75
Thomas Kempton House
60 Thomas Street
c1775
Private

Continue one block south on Pleasant Street to Maxfield Street and turn right. Drive up Maxfield Street to Thomas Street and turn left. The Thomas Kempton House is the third house on the left.

Thomas Kempton was a British soldier, Colonial Minuteman, descendant of an original landowner, and leader of men. Two days after the "shot heard round the world"[18] was fired at Lexington and Concord in April of 1775, Captain Kempton was outside literally building this house for his family. A

164

Thomas Kempton House

speeding rider brought him the fateful news. He immediately told his wife she would have to manage without him, grabbed his musket, alerted his company of Minutemen, and was on the road for Roxbury. Within the next few days 20,000 men assembled around Boston in a valiant attempt to defeat the British at the Battle of Bunker Hill at Breed's Hill. The initial shock of Concord and Lexington brought on an almost fanatical response of do or die, to leave the plow and fight for liberty. Unfortunately, there was also the general naive feeling that it would be a short skirmish, with an early victory, and all would be home by harvest time. Little did these eager defenders know the war would last five, long, cold, grueling years, with many a defeat before final victory at Yorktown.

The Kempton name goes back to Manasseh Kempton, one of the thirty-six purchasers of the Dartmouth tract in 1652. His main section of land was bordered by today's Spring Street, Rockdale Avenue, Sycamore Street, and the Acushnet River. Having no children, he willed the lands to a nephew, Manasseh Kempton of Long Island, who sold the land between Elm and Sycamore Streets to cousin Ephraim III, and to brother Samuel the land between Spring and Elm Streets. Samuel never lived on his land but sold to Captain Samuel Willis, who in turn sold to Joseph Russell, grandfather of Joseph Russell III, founder of New Bedford. The land on Thomas Street, where the present Kempton House now stands, was passed down from Ephraim III to grandson Thomas Kempton.

Thomas Kempton, born in 1740, had an interesting and varied life. He was a master mariner in the coastal trade, a navigator on the sloop *Diamond* and in 1765 Captain of the sloop *Dove*. In 1773 he received a commission in the British service, which he subsequently resigned in favor of the local patriot cause. At the outbreak of hostilities he was a captain of the militia, where many of its members had served under him aboard ship. A well-liked and adroit commander, he was promoted to Lieutenant Colonel before he retired from active service in 1776 due to ill health. He continued to serve his young community as selectman, assessor, and later as teacher of navigation and math. Also, with improved health, he returned to his first love, the sea, as captain of the sloop *Polly*.

Colonel Kempton died in 1806, leaving this house to his son, William, who in turn left it to daughter Harriet, who lived here until her death in 1841. She was the last of the line of direct descent from the historic Kempton name. Today the house is a rooming house and gives little evidence of its historic past.

#76
Marine Park
Popes Island
Route 6, Fairhaven Bridge
Open all year, no fee

Return on Thomas Street to Maxfield Street, turn left and go to County Street. Turn left on County and follow it to Kempton Street, Route 6, and turn left. Follow Route 6 over the bridge to Fairhaven. After entering the bridge area take the second right to Marine Park. Facilities: picnicking, fishing, fishing party boat rental, parking.

Marine Park offers a quiet oasis in the midst of the busy harbor and a chance to enjoy a panoramic view of the entire inner harbor. Popes Island has a small rocky breakwater and narrow beach — inviting to walk along, study the vista, and enjoy the perspective. A charter boat is available at the small dock.

On the right you can spot the Coast Guard Lightship *New Bedford,** the fish and scallop auction house called Wharfinger's* on one side, and the huge State Pier* on the other. Just inland is the Whaling Museum* dominating Johnny Cake Hill

166

and reminiscent of the ancient waterfront scene. South of State Pier* are Homer's and Leonard's Wharves.* Farther south is the South Terminal area and its fish processing plants. And everywhere are fishing boats.

Directly south you can clearly see the Hurricane Barrier* and Palmer Island Lighthouse.* Watch boats heading out through the barrier or coming home from the Banks. On the left, Fairhaven church steeples and radio towers, along with masts of fishing boats, are all reflected in the waters of the inner harbor.

BLACK HERITAGE TRAIL

BACKGROUND

"New Bedford is a good place for Blacks ... a good place where all races get along with each other ... not like other cities. We have a pluralistic society where we share and value each other's distinct cultures, not a melting pot."[19] These comments of modern New Bedford Blacks have been echoed by their predecessors through the centuries as far back as before the American Revolution. For "the cultural heritage and contributions of the Blacks, Indians, and Cape Verdeans to New Bedford's growth and development"[20] began before there was a United States and continue today.

Blacks have been part of the whaling adventure since its earliest days when nearly half the crew were Black. New Bedford has drawn her Black heritage from freed slaves and free seamen from continental Africa, the Cape Verdean Islands, and the islands of the Carribbean. Some married Indians or Whites, adding to the racial and cultural variety. Possibly the long existence of different racial and ethnic groups in New Bedford accounts for the good feelings of today. The distrust of the unknown and threat to job security usually connected with the arrival of a new ethnic group were not present here. Though new immigrants continue to arrive, their predecessors have already proved there is room for all.

New Bedford, led by her Quaker citizens, has long been staunchly against slavery. In 1772 action began with Quaker pressure on individuals who held slaves, and by 1785 they could report that there were no evidences of any slavery in New Bedford. New Bedford was an important part of the Underground Railroad aimed at aiding Blacks to escape slavery to freedom in the north. Underground was not necessarily an appropriate description, however, as New Bedford Blacks walked tall and openly and did not need the usual tunnels and other hiding places as did other "stations" along the way. Aid to escaping slaves was not usually recorded, as it violated fugitive slave laws, but it is safe to conclude that many escapees were helped by Quaker-led Whites as well as already established New Bedford Blacks.

FAMOUS SONS AND DAUGHTERS

New Bedford is proud of her famous sons and daughters of Black heritage. Sergeant William H. Carney was the first Black to be awarded the Congressional Medal of Honor. This New Bedford man volunteered to join the Union Army, as a member of the United States Colored Troops, the 54th Massachusetts, Company C from New Bedford. On July 18, 1863, during the battle at Fort Wagner in South Carolina, Sergeant Carney demonstrated the loyalty and bravery which won him the coveted medal. As the flagman fell during the third assault, Carney grabbed the flag and held it high. The flag was the communication signal; the men followed the raised flag, while a fallen flag often signalled retreat or disorganization. Carney carried the flag through the bullet-ridden battle, though he was wounded three times. He later collapsed, but first reported, "Boys, the old flag never touched the ground."[21] Like the immortalized flag-raising scene at Iwo Jima nearly a century later, Carney's heroic actions set the stage for later victory.

Sergeant Carney's 1852 homestead has been restored and is maintained by the owner, the Martha E. Briggs Educational Club.

Frederick Douglass, noted orator, author, publisher, religious leader, and political reformer for human rights, began his career and lived here in his first years as a freeman. Said Douglass: "My first afternoon on reaching New Bedford, was spent in visiting the wharves and viewing the shipping. The sight of the broad brim and the plain Quaker dress, which met me at every turn, greatly increased my sense of freedom and security. I am among the Quakers, thought I, and am safe ... On wharves I saw industry without bustle, labor without noise, and heavy toil without the whip."[22]

Much earlier, Paul Cuffe, son of a freed slave and his Wampanoag Indian wife, became a great mariner, prosperous trader, shipbuilder and owner, real estate investor, and political leader. Born in 1759, he profited from the combined education of his African father and American Indian relatives' sharing their valuable knowledge of the land and sea, and the Quakers who

Sergeant William H. Carney House

taught him navigation and the technology of the sea. He worked
on his father's one-hundred-acre farm on Cuttyhunk Island and
then signed on as a whaleman for several long voyages. Here he
first saw the terrible reality of a slave ship and began his personal
protest for equal human rights. He led a group of Blacks and Indians in a protest against taxation without voting rights. As a
result, by 1783 Blacks who were taxed were also eligible to vote.
He pioneered the colonization by Afro-American freemen of a
small colony on the West Coast of Africa. In New Bedford, when
he saw the need of a school, he built it and hired the teacher. A
Quaker, he helped build a new meetinghouse. William Rotch,
Jr., a leading whaling entrepeneur of the day, was a business
associate and personal friend. Rotch probably aided Cuffe in his
philanthropic activities with the school and meetinghouse and
supported his mercantile efforts as well. The story is told of the
time that the host of a public house was offering separate seating
to Paul Cuffe and was interrupted by William Rotch, Jr., who
had invited Cuffe to dine and led him to Rotch's own table.

Lewis Temple in 1848 perfected the toggle harpoon, called
the most significant innovation in the history of whaling. It is also
known as the Temple iron. Elizabeth Carter Brooks, since her
childhood, was dedicated to helping the elderly. She founded the
first New Bedford Home for the Aged in 1897 before she had
even graduated from Normal School. Daughter of a freed slave,

Mrs. Brooks was a teacher for twenty-seven years, a noted lecturer, an organizer of Black women's clubs, and active in church and community affairs. At the turn of the century, Dr. Juan Drummond became the first Black woman doctor in Southeastern Massachusetts.

Bishop Charles M. Grace, also known as "Sweet Daddy" Grace, was a striking, magnetic, eloquent evangelist. Born in the Cape Verde Islands in 1881, he began his evangelism in New Bedford and established the "House of Prayer for All People" on Kempton Street. It became the mother church of the 350 others he established throughout the country. He purportedly died a multi-millionaire.

Mrs. Jane C. Waters, local educator, designed the original Black Heritage Trail in conjunction with the Bicentennial celebration and wrote a booklet for it. Her son, Herbert R. Waters, Jr., is the principal of Carney Academy and the first Black to receive the rank of colonel in the Marine Corps Reserves. Joli Gonsalves, of Cape Verdean descent, is an internationally known baritone, speaks twenty-eight languages, and now has a three-language television show called "Cape Verdeans."

THE BLACK HERITAGE TRAIL

Lewis Temple's Blacksmith Shop site — 3 Walnut Street

Liberty Bell Plaque — Memorial of the bell rung by abolitionist Mayor Rodney French to warn slaves of approaching US marshalls; corner Purchase and William Streets, east wall of Merchants National Bank.

Whaleman Statue — The important harpooner was often Black as were nearly half the crew; New Bedford Free Public Library*, Pleasant and William Streets.

Frederick Douglass Plaque — Inside the New Bedford Free Public Library*, Pleasant and William Streets.

Memorial to Cape Verdean Military Servicemen — 561 Purchase Street.

Grave sites of Lewis Temple and Nathan Johnson* — Rural Cemetery, Rockdale Avenue between Grape and Dartmouth.

Rodney French Plaque — In honor of the abolitionist mayor of New Bedford; entrance to Hazelwood Park* on West Rodney French Boulevard.

New Bedford Home for the Aged — Founded by Elizabeth Carter Brooks; 396 Middle Street.

House of Prayer for All People — 419 Kempton Street.

Sergeant William H. Carney Home — 128 Mill Street.

Monument to Black Service Men and Women — Buttonwood Park*, Rockdale Avenue near Kempton Street.

Douglass Memorial A.M.E. Zion Church — 600 Kempton Street.

ANNUAL FESTIVALS AND EVENTS
Public invited, no entrance fees

Rediscovery Days — July 4th Weekend

Parades, fireworks, and traditional Independence Day entertainments are joined by crafts and arts fairs, seafood, ethnic food, walking tours, harbor cruises, road and sail races during this four-day celebration.

Whaling City Festival — Weekend following July 4th

Centered at Buttonwood Park*, the four-day Whaling City Festival features a flea market, movies, art, crafts, music, sporting events, food, and other special events and entertainments.

Feast of the Blessed Sacrament — Usually first weekend in August

This annual Portugese festival was originally a religious thanksgiving celebration and continues to be. A mass and proces-

Scenes from The Madeira Feast

sion are held at the Church of Our Lady of the Immaculate Conception at Earle and Dinan Streets in connection with the festival which is centered at the Medeira Field Grounds a block away. The festival includes ethnic and American music and foods, games, rides, a midway, and fireworks.

Seafood Heritage Days — Time varies, late July or early August, sometimes combined with other festivals

The Downtown Mall is the scene of combined business and fishing interests paying tribute to the fishing industry, long such a vital part of New Bedford. Displays of fishing related equipment, demonstrations and contests of fish filleting and cooking combine with food and entertainment during Seafood Heritage Days.

Blessing of the Fleet — Second weekend in August, recently in conjunction with the Centre Street Festival

The New Bedford Fishermen's Wives sponsor this colorful annual happening held at the State Pier. The event is highlighted by the parade of the fishing fleet and includes music and services of thanksgiving.

Centre Street Festival — Usually second weekend in August

The flavor of the Waterfront Historic District comes alive with this craftsmen's fair. Scrimshanders (makers of scrimshaw art), woodworkers, weavers, potters, silversmiths — members of many of the old New England special hand crafts — give demonstrations. The Centre Street setting and other historic displays combine with entertainments, including music, food, and activities for all.

Centre Street Festival

MAJOR PUBLIC PARKS
Public invited, no entrance fees

Park	Facilities
Brooklawn Park Acushnet Avenue and Ashley Boulevard	Picnicking, tennis, ball fields, playground, ice skating, rest rooms, parking
Buttonwood Park* Rockdale Avenue and Hawthorn Street	Zoo, greenhouse, refreshments, rest rooms, tennis, playground, ball fields, paddleboats, train rides, ice skating, fishing, picnicking, parking
Commons Pearl, Purchase, County, Pope Streets	Playground equipment, benches, pretty view
Hazelwood Park* W. Rodney French Boulevard	Picnicking, bowling on the green, tennis, basketball courts, tot playground, fields, pretty view, rest rooms, parking
Marine Park* Popes Island, Route 6, Fairhaven Bridge	Picnicking, fishing, fishing party boat rental, parking, harbor view
Flora B. Pierce Nature Trail New Plainville Road	Picnicking, nature walks, bird watching, wildlife study, hiking, fishing, boating, parking

Directions: For access, go north on Cottage Street which becomes Mt. Pleasant. Continue on Mt. Pleasant into New Plainville Road where, just after Shawmut Avenue, there is a parking area

on the right. **Next on the right is Turner's Pond with the signed entrance to the Nature Trail across from the pond on the left.**

A map at the entrance describes the trails and terrain of this natural sanctuary, once part of the scene of early saw mills located on man-made Turner's Pond. Well marked trails, with bridges over the stream, and marsh areas protected by raised wood paths, lead into the pleasant, wooded wilderness and open fields. Example trees are marked with their English and Latin names. A haven for animals and birds, the low marsh lands of Cedar Swamp are the source of the Paskamansett River, which flows from Turner's Pond for ten miles to Buzzards Bay and the open sea.

FOOTNOTES

1 (page 19) Bullard, John M., *The Rotches,* Milford, N.H.: W.B. and A.R. Rotch Cabinet Press, 1947, p. 14.

2 (page 24) The main source of information on the Arctic came from: Allen, Everett S., *Children of the Light,* Boston: Little, Brown and Co., 1973.

3 (page 26) *Historic Building Survey,* Office of Historic Preservation, p. 2.

4 (page 28) The main source of information came from: Bullard, John K., *Ten Acrevival,* Thesis, MIT, 1974.

5 (page 34) Melville, Herman, *Moby Dick,* New York: Random House, 1950, p. 32-33.

6 (page 51) Entrance sign, Seamen's Bethel, New Bedford.

7 (page 52) Melville, Herman, *Moby Dick,* New York: Random House, 1950, p. 33.

8 (page 53) New Bedford Port Society booklet, p. 1.

9 (page 77) Ellis, Leonard B., *History of New Bedford and Its Vicinity, 1602-1892,* Syracuse, N.Y.: D. Mason and Co., 1892, Biography Section, p. 26.

10 (page 84) Forbes, A., and J.W. Greene, *Rich Men of Massachusetts,* Boston: Petridge and Company, 1851, p. 190.

11 (page 124) Forbes, A. and J.W. Greene, *Rich Men of Massachusetts,* Boston: Petridge and Company, 1851, p. 190.

12 (page 134) *Standard-Times,* New Bedford, Massachusetts, April 10, 1967.

13 (page 136) Ricketson, Daniel, *New Bedford of the Past,* Cambridge: Houghton, Mifflin and Co., 1903, p. 156.

14 (page 140) *Standard-Times,* New Bedford, Massachusetts, Jan. 4, 1925.

15 (page 159) *Standard-Times,* New Bedford, Massachusetts, Dec. 11, 1957.

16 (page 160) *Standard-Times,* New Bedford, Massachusetts, Feb. 18, 1937.

17 (page 161) Sparkes, Boyden, and Samuel Taylor Moore, *The Witch of Wall Street* Hetty Green, New York: Doubleday, 1935.

18 (page 164) Matthews, Brander, editor, *Poems of American Patriotism,* New York: Charles Scribner's Sons, 1922, p. 18.

19 (page 168) Interviews with Herbert R. Waters, Jr. and Joli Gonsalves.

20 (page 168) Waters, Jane, *Black Heritage Trail,* New Bedford: 1976, p. II.

21 (page 169) Sgt. William H. Carney Memorial Academy Dedication and Open House booklet, 1977.

22 (page 169) Waters, Jane, *Black Heritage Trail,* New Bedford: 1976, p. 10.

BIBLIOGRAPHY

Allen, Everett S., *Children of the Light,* Boston: Little, Brown and Co., 1973.

Allen, Everett S., *A Wind to Shake the World,* Boston: Little, Brown and Co., 1976.

America's Forgotten Architecture, National Trust for Historic Preservation, Pantheon, 1976.

Anthony, Joseph, *Life in New Bedford A Hundred Years Ago* (from his diary), New Bedford, Mass.: George H. Reynolds Pub., 1922.

Bearse, Ray, editor, *Massachusetts: A Guide to the Pilgrim State,* Boston: Houghton Mifflin Co., 1971.

Berchen, William, and Monica Dickens, *Cape Cod,* New York: Viking Press, 1972.

Bruce, Curt, and Jill Grossman, *Revelations of New England Architecture* People and Their Buildings, New York: Grossman Publishers, Division of Viking Press, 1975.

Bullard, John K., *Ten Acrevival,* Thesis, MIT, 1974.

Bullard, John M., *Friends' Academy,* New Bedford, Mass.: Reynolds-DeWalt Printers, 1960.

Bullard, John M., *The Rotches,* Milford, N.H.: W.B. and A.R. Rotch Cabinet Press, 1947.

Carpenter, Allan, *Enchantment of America Massachusetts,* Chicago: Childrens Press, 1965.

Chamberlain, Samuel, *The New England Image,* New York: Hastings House, 1963.

Colby, Jean Poindexter, *Plimoth Plantation Then and Now,* New York: Hastings House, 1974.

Commemorative Guide to the Massachusetts Bicentennial, Yankee Inc., 1975.

Demos, John, *A Little Commonwealth,* Family Life in Plymouth Colony, New York: Oxford University Press, 1970.

Diary of Reverend Moses How, Series of Sketches of New Bedford's Early History, #59, Reynolds Printing.

Dickinson, Alice, *The Colony of Massachusetts*, New York: Franklin Watts, Inc., 1975.

Ellis, Leonard Bolles, *History of New Bedford and Its Vicinity 1602-1892*, Syracuse, N.Y.: D. Mason and Co., 1892.

Emery, William M., *An Historical Sketch.*

Federal Writers' Project, *Fairhaven Massachusetts*, American Guide Series, Fairhaven, Mass., 1939.

Ferro, Maximilian L., *How to Love and Care for Your Old Building in New Bedford*, New Bedford, Mass.: Office of Historic Preservation, 1977.

Fitch, James Marston, *American Building*, Boston: Houghton Mifflin, 1948.

Forbes, A., and J.W. Greene, *Rich Men of Massachusetts*, Boston: Petridge and Company, 1851.

Genealogy Room, New Bedford Free Public Library, unpublished files.

Hawes, William L., *New Bedford in the China Trade*, 1940.

Hawke, David, *Colonial Experience*, New York: Bobbs-Merrill Co. Inc., 1966.

Hegarty, Reginald B., *New Bedford and American Whaling*, New Bedford: Reynolds Printing Co., 1960.

Hegarty, Reginald B., *New Bedford's History*, New Bedford: Reynolds Printing Co., 1959.

Historic American Buildings Survey, Scribner Historic Buildings Series, New York: Charles Scribner's and Sons, 1976.

Jones, Charles Henry, *Genealogy of Rodman Family 1620-1886*, Philadelphia: Allen, Lane & Scott, 1886.

Matthews, Brander, editor, *Poems of American Patriotism*, New York: Charles Scribner's Sons, 1922.

Melville, Herman, *Moby Dick*, New York: Random House, 1950.

Miller, John C., *First Frontier, Life in Colonial America*, New York: Bell Publishing Co., 1975.

Morison, Samuel Eliot, *Builders of the Bay Colony*, Boston: Houghton Mifflin Co., 1964.

Morgan, Edmund S., *The Puritan Dilemma*, Boston: Little, Brown and Company, 1958.

New Bedford, Massachusetts Its History, Industries, Institutions, and Attractions, New Bedford: Board of Trade, Mercury Publishing Co., 1889.

New Bedford Monthly Meetings 1792-1892, New Bedford: E. Anthony & Sons, Inc.

New Bedford and Old Dartmouth: A Portrait of a Region's Past, New Bedford: Bicentennial Exhibition of Old Dartmouth Historical Society at the Whaling Museum, 1975.

New Bedford Waterfront, New Bedford, Massachusetts, A Coastal City in Transition, Cambridge: Harvard Graduate School of Design, Community Assistance Program, 1977.

Pamphlets on New Bedford, mainly Reynolds Printing Co.

Pease, Zephaniah W., *History of New Bedford,* Vol. I, II, III, New York: Lewis Historical Publishing Co., 1918.

Pease, Zephaniah W., *One Hundredth Anniversary of the New Bedford Port Society,* 1830-1930, Historical address reprinted from *The Morning Mercury.*

Photographs of Houses and Public Buildings in New Bedford, and surrounding area, bound typescript, notes Henry B. Worth, editor Emma C. Austin, photographer Fred W. Palmer, Old Dartmouth Historical Society Library, 1907.

Pierce, James Smith, *From Abacus to Zeus,* Englewood Cliffs, N.J.: Prentice-Hall, Inc., 1968.

Preservation and Rehabilitation of a Historic Commercial Area, study by New Bedford Redevelopment Authority, City Planning Office, WHALE, New Bedford, 1960s.

Representative Men and Old Families of Southeastern Massachusetts, Chicago: J.H. Beers and Co., 1912.

Ricketson, Daniel, *History of New Bedford,* New Bedford: 1858.

Ricketson, Daniel, *New Bedford of the Past,* Cambridge: Houghton, Mifflin and Co., 1903.

Rodman, Julia W., *The History* (Grace Episcopal Church)

Rotch, William, *Memorandum* written by author, 1916.

Russell, Barrett Beard, *The Descendants of John Russell of Dartmouth, Massachusetts,* reprinted from New England Historical and Genealogical Register Vols. 58, 59, Boston, 1904, 1915.

Rutman, Darrett B., *John Winthrop's Decision for America: 1629,* Philadelphia: J.B. Lippincott Co., 1975.

Short History of the First Unitarian Church, New Bedford, Massachusetts, 1708-1958.

Smith, G.E. Kidder, *Pictorial History of Architecture in America,* Vol. I, II, New York: American Heritage Pub. Co. Inc., 1976.

Snow, Edward Rowe, *The Lighthouses of New England,* New York: Dodd, Mead & Company, 1973.

Sparkes, Boyden, and Samuel Taylor Moore, *The Witch of Wall Street* Hetty Green, New York: Doubleday, 1935.

Standard-Times, New Bedford, Massachusetts, various weekday and Sunday issues.

Stevens, William O., *Nantucket the Far Away Island,* New York: Dodd, Mead & Company, 1966.

Waters, Jane, *Black Heritage Trail,* New Bedford: 1976.

Whiffen, Marcus, *American Architecture Since 1780* A Guide to the Styles, Cambridge: MIT Press, 1969.

Williams, Henry Lionell, and Ottalie K. Williams, *Old American Houses 1700-1850,* New York, Bonanza Books, 1967.

Williams, Winston, *Nantucket Then and Now,* New York: Dodd, Mead & Company, 1977.

INDEX